—— The ——
DENVILLE 13

The DENVILLE 13

MURDER, REDEMPTION & FORGIVENESS IN SMALL-TOWN NEW JERSEY

PETER ZABLOCKI

THE
History
PRESS

Published by The History Press
Charleston, SC
www.historypress.com

Front: Denville town center, circa 1950s. *Courtesy of the Denville Historical Society.*

First published 2021

Manufactured in the United States

ISBN 9781467148344

Library of Congress Control Number: 2020945778

Notice: The information in this book is true and complete to the best of our knowledge. It is offered without guarantee on the part of the author or The History Press. The author and The History Press disclaim all liability in connection with the use of this book.

For all my students—past, present and future. May they always remember to learn from their mistakes and never forget the hidden strength of forgiveness.

P.Z.

CONTENTS

PREFACE

This, at its core, is a cautionary tale. It is also a story of the pitfalls of youth and the struggle of the citizenry to fulfill its responsibility for the moral training of its young people. It is a tale of mistakes, regrets, unfortunate circumstance and, above all, forgiveness and redemption. It is not a pretty tale, and it is one that I have wrestled with since I first decided to research it and write about it. My intent from the start was to provide the most objective historical account of events as they transpired. While the research took months of extensive work, it was the latter that proved to be the bigger challenge.

I first came across the events researched in this book while conducting separate research on Denville during World War II. During my interviews about the 1940s and war experiences with the town's senior citizen population, I was told, on a few occasions, about a murder that had occurred in Denville in the 1950s. While it was not my intent to research said event, the frequency of the topic coming up in my interviews and the quaint way in which it was mentioned to me on each occasion led me to this work. I thought, and still do, that out of respect for those involved who are still alive, as well as their family members and the town of Denville itself, publishing the following work should not be taken lightly. It is also the reason why I chose to exclude certain images and the last names of those directly involved. Yet, as I wrestled with this particular aspect of my town's history, my thought kept on returning to my own sons, who will soon be the same age as the boys who grace the pages of this story. It was with them in mind that I decided to uncover a case that has inevitably shaped the town of Denville into the great community it is today. It is, as mentioned before, a cautionary tale of the impulsiveness of youth and the effects that transient decisions have on the rest of our lives, as well as those of our families and our communities.

Denville, New Jersey, is a small town known for its family friendly atmosphere and amazing community. Yet as this research will show, it does also have darker stories to tell. The only surviving file of the *Denville Herald*, Denville's newspaper from the 1930s to the 1950s—located in the Denville Public Library in a PDF format and in the Denville Historical Society on microfilm—mysteriously omits the pages referring to the following event. While it was widely reported throughout the state and the nation, the people of Denville have chosen to move on from it. In fact, all signs point to the event being deliberately, respectfully and painstakingly hidden in plain sight for over seventy years. I think that we should be proud of our small communities and realize that they have been created from the successes, as well as the hardships and failures, of those who came before us.

As such, I worried that, with today's penchant for true crime and social media, the story would come out sooner or later and for the wrong reasons. I saw it as my duty to the town that I call home to tell a story that hopefully provides enough objectivity and justice to all those involved. It might even vindicate some who have been shamed by others who silently continue to mention the event today without having much perspective or knowledge of what actually transpired. Maybe by bringing this case into the open, we can finally put it to rest and stop the quiet murmurs and rumors that have tormented not only all those involved but also the small town for the past seventy years. Likewise, I hope that young people can take advantage of learning from other people's mistakes without having to make them themselves.

Peter Zablocki
Denville Historical Society
Denville, New Jersey
February 20, 2020

ACKNOWLEDGEMENTS

First and foremost, I would love to thank my best friend, constant supporter and the person who never fails to push me to be the best version of myself, my wife. She has read numerous drafts of this work, providing suggestions and honest advice along the way. If you enjoy this story, it is because of her, and if you do not, it is because I did not fully heed her advice. I would also like to thank everyone on the board of the Denville Historical Society for welcoming me to their family a few years back and trusting me with the research of our amazing town's history. Thank you for the support and guidance of Vito Bianco, the man who knows so much about Denville's history that he probably forgot more about it than I could ever dream of learning myself. I would also like to thank the people who read the early drafts of this work and provided pointers, advice, objectivity and food for thought, all of which allowed me to create the work that you now hold in your hands: Kristin Nieto, Mary Miraldi, Christopher Wagner, Maryellen Liddy, Vincent Shivas and Jess Bentley.

Thank you to Thomas C. Schmid, assistant prosecutor at the Morris County Prosecutor's Office, who granted me access to the files on which a large portion of this work is based. Likewise, thank you to the late Bob Illig, who had the interest, the drive and the premonition to collect the initial newspaper clippings that began this research.

INTRODUCTION

The story of the Denville 13 revealed itself to historians while conducting research on the town of Denville during World War II. As one of the town historians conducted interviews with people who were around in the 1930s and 1940s, on more than one occasion, he was told of a murder that took place in the town in the early 1950s. While the topic came up on four different occasions, with four different people, what connected all the occurrences was how it was mentioned. In all four cases, the reference to the murder came up after the recording device for the interview was off. One interviewee even asked if it was off before proceeding to mention it. What followed could be described more like an uncovering of the event than a simple research into the past. In fact, in today's digital age, it should not have been as challenging as it was to reconstruct the events of that fateful August day. Why was this not mentioned before? Why do people living in town not know about it? Why do those who do know about it never speak of it out loud? Perhaps the answers lie in the simple fact that it was meant to be forgotten—and perhaps deliberately designed to stay that way.

Rebel Without a Cause (1955), the movie that posthumously propelled James Dean to stardom, was, at the time of its release, a social commentary on the decade's fear of juvenile delinquency and teen angst. With the rise of television, comic books and radio, the American youth of the decade was being accused of becoming too disconnected from their parents' values and desensitized to violence and vice. Yet some of these fears, which by 1954, called for Senate subcommittee hearings to come up with solutions, were not always unfounded. Sometimes, the fear, and the reality behind it, hit a little too close to home.

"Man Found Slain in Lover's Lane in Denville," read the headline plastered all over a local newspaper from Monday, August 31, 1953.[1] Late that day, charges were expected to be filed in Morris County Court in Morristown against nine suspects held in connection with the brutal "sex-slaying" the day before. And then, as if from a scene from the Senate hearings on juvenile delinquency, within days, the same newspaper reported, "13 to Be Arraigned for Murder; Those Accused Range in Age from 14 to 22." Accordingly, and as per the grand jury report from October of the same year, Denville had become the scene of the largest number of persons ever indicted for one murder in the entire nation up to that point.[2] So, what happened on that infamous Saturday night of August 29, 1953? Nearly seventy years later, perhaps the most infamous night in the town's short history has been all but forgotten. But why is that?

A simple Google search into the murder in Denville in 1950s did not yield any results. Looking through the Denville archives in the Denville Historical Society and Museum led to short newspaper clippings about the murder, which provided the first major clue: its date. Even knowing the date did not help with the internet search. Then there were the newspaper clippings themselves. The excerpts were cut out and placed in a binder in the Illig collection at the town's museum. Bob Illig was a freelance historian of the town from the 1970s to his death in the early 2000s. His research—hours of recorded interviews and volumes of collected newspaper clippings, picture collections, written histories and more—makes up a large portion of the museum's collection and was the natural first place to look. The problem remained that the couple newspaper clippings were not labeled with the newspapers from which they came. At first, this did not seem like it was going to be a problem, as Denville had its own newspaper at the time of the murder, the *Denville Herald*. A national news story, as the Denville 13 murder was, would, for sure, make the front page of the town's newspaper. It had to be the origin of the newspaper clipping.

Accessing the PDF scan of the entire twenty-plus-year run of the town's newspaper did not come up with anything about the murder. The *Herald* was released weekly on Thursdays, so the closest print date to the murder would have to be September 3, 1953—three days after it took place. Yet there is no mention of it; rather, there is no evidence of it ever being there. Out of the thousands of scanned pages, the digital collection of the newspaper is complete, minus one full year in the 1930s and the first three pages of the September 3, 1953 edition. But maybe it was just a coincidence.

The next step was powering up an old microfilm machine at the Denville Museum and going to the original microfilm collection of the town newspaper, collected by the Morris County Library in the 1970s. After finally getting the film going and moving the reel to September 3, 1953, it was discovered that the entire issue from that week was missing. Not to be undone, the researcher turned to an invaluable source at the museum, namely the crates with the original weekly newspapers. Handling them with care, the historian searched through the hard copies of the newspapers, and it was apparent that the newspapers, while very old, were placed meticulously in the right order by whoever collected them. With each turn of yet another issue, one could feel the excitement. But then, after picking up the August 27, 1953 edition, the researcher's gaze fell on the *Denville Herald* issue of September 10, 1953. The elusive September 3 edition was still nowhere to be found.

The next step was researching nearby newspapers that would also serve Denville during the time, *Mountain Lakes News*, the *Madison Eagle*, *Boonton Times* and the *Citizen of Morris County*. Interestingly, none of them mention the crime, which at the time, was the largest indictment for a single murder in American history. How is that possible? After visiting the history department at the Morristown Public Library in Morristown, New Jersey, the search finally paid off. Morristown is what could be considered the closest large city to Denville, New Jersey. It is also the county seat of Morris County, acting as its administrative center and seat of government. As such, its newspaper, the *Daily Record*, which was published daily, as opposed to weekly as in other smaller towns in Morris County, was the closest small county towns would get to big-city reporting and news. The *Daily Record* carried the story on its front page. As far as real reporting goes, it placed aside any feelings, reservations and/or discreteness the small town of Denville might have had or desired about the issue. For the next few months, the paper also carried the most complete reporting on the crime perhaps in the whole county.

Once the major players, dates, names and details were found in Morristown's *Daily Record*, the story started to unravel a bit more. Searching through commercial access newspaper databases, the *New York Times* and newsapers.com made it apparent exactly how big of a story this was on a national scale. In fact, the event was reported as far as Ohio, Florida and the Carolinas. Ironically, it received more coverage in Virginia than the town and county in which the event took place. There had to be a reason for this. It might be a very obvious one. After all, Denville was, and still is, a very small, family-oriented, friendly town. In a pamphlet published in the 1960s, titled *Why Choose Denville*, people from all walks of life were courted to move to the town for its cheerful, activity-filled and lake-relaxing atmosphere. A murder such as the one that happened in 1953 would only hurt the community that still relied on out-of-towners to spend money at various town center stores and summer lake communities. Additionally, the 1950s were the biggest housing boom in the town's short history up to that point—something that would likely be stalled if the news of the murder really caught the attention of the media. As such, it became something that was just not talked about. Seemingly out of respect for the quaint town, the nearby townships also chose to not run the story. As this research shows, this mission to forget it continued for many years after—even when many of those who could remember it had themselves passed away.

1
SEEDS OF DISSENT

Ten years—almost to the day—before the events that grace the pages of this book took place, the small and peaceful town of Denville, New Jersey, found itself amid the national trend of rising juvenile crime rates. The township of about 3,100 residents spent the summer of 1943 holding committee meetings to study and gain advice and recommendations on the problems of youth delinquency. Led by a chairman of the department of public safety, Joseph Chappell, the organization asked citizens for advice on what was seen as one of the most concerning issues of the town at the time. This was quite an interesting claim, as during the same months that the meetings took place, the world was deep into the Second World War, with American soldiers having just invaded Italy and sustaining staggering casualties. On the day of the first juvenile delinquency panel meeting in July 1943, the town's Honor Roll in the center of town, which provided the names of all Denville men and women who fought in the war, was temporarily opened, and another three names were added, bringing the total to 262. Yet, curiously, the citizens of the town seemed to be more concerned with what was happening right here with the youth left behind.

Wartime, which sees conscription numbers at an all-time high, strains family values and even the social fabric of any nation, and World War II was no exception. Young people in Denville found themselves without proper supervision as they witnessed their fathers and older siblings being drafted into the armed forces and their mothers entering wartime jobs that were, up to this point, reserved for men. Even for teenagers, wartime jobs were aplenty—a refreshing change from the Great Depression years that had proceeded it. As such, teenagers all of a sudden acquired part-time jobs and pay that, awhile back, they could only dream of. With these changes came feelings of neglect for some and newfound freedom and even entitlement for others.

The Children's Bureau of the United States Department of Labor compiles juvenile court statistics from major cities, and its findings from wartime years reveal a growing trend of young men landing before the court of law. In comparison to 1938, by 1944, boys' cases had grown by a staggering 51 percent.[3] Concurrently, the Federal Bureau of Investigation is privy to fingerprints from all local and state police authorities, which also point to the sharp rise in juvenile delinquency. For instance, in 1943, the FBI saw a 23 percent rise in cases of boys under the age of eighteen who were fingerprinted; by 1944, it rose another 21 percent.[4] The Denville cases, however, have one major difference, which provides context to the events that transpired ten years later—the age of the perpetrators.

The *Denville Herald* reported, "Maybe you've thought juvenile delinquency is a problem for large cities, with congested populations and slum districts, to worry about while suburban-rural areas like Denville could rely on beneficent effects of green grass and plenty of sunlight to take care of youth problems. Then think again, as those who have legal and moral obligations toward the social health of Denville are doing."[5] The local newspaper article calling for action to meet the problem of juvenile delinquency was quick to point out that there was not a juvenile crime wave in the small town or that anybody was thinking about establishing a curfew. Yet it did acknowledge that there was a problem, in fact, a unique problem.

Police Chief Harry B. Jenkins, reviewing the situation, pointed out that "within the past 6 months he had investigated cases like these: Tabor action, house damaged to the extent of $150; Indian Lake stores, damage of $90 to $170; Indian Lake Club House, $20 to $25; Cedar Lake, $20–$25; miscellaneous destruction of street and highway signs, broken street lights, and other malicious mischief where consequences can't be assessed in terms of money but are nevertheless real to the owners."[6] For reference, the average hourly wage at the time was $0.30 per hour. But then came this: "It may be surprising to those who are accustomed to thinking of such acts in connection with 'teenage' youngsters, but Chief Jenkins says the majority of the damage mentioned was done by kids up to 11 years old. The house in Tabor section, for instance, was wrecked by three miscreants, 6, 7, and 8 years old."[7]

Small-town charm was apparent in Denville during the 1951 town fair, which benefited the Denville Fire Department. *Denville Historical Society.*

Just as they would again in 1953, the Denville townsfolk attempted to find the answers to what was corrupting their youngest citizens. According to Chief Jenkins, the biggest factor, and probably the most obvious and easiest to point to, was the employment of parents in war work. Jenkins went as far as pointing out that he knew of cases in which both parents were working, sometimes on overlapping shifts, and the children were left without any guidance or supervision for most of the day and night. These were children as young as five years old. "It's a job for the school and parents," he said, adding that the police did not have much chance until the damage was already done.[8] "I think the answer lies in more teaching of good citizenship and more interest on the part of parents. I seriously question the wisdom of parents being so tied up in war work that they neglect their young children."

While the police chief praised the schools for doing a magnificent job in safety education, he did ask them to come up with some other solutions to the growing problem. Still, he was very much zeroed in on the parents as the root cause. With what one might find eerie irony, Jenkins commented, "I doubt whether the production gained when a mother leaves her home and children to take a war job equals the damage done to our future citizens down the line." In another reference to things to come, the chief acknowledged that while he had no special trouble with "sex cases," he would not be surprised if "things develop in that direction too."[9] He added, "After all, children in Denville probably aren't so very much different than they are in other places, and if other places have that problem we probably have some too."

Reverend Charles Mead of the Denville Community Church—which would once again provide the stage for discussion on the issue of juvenile delinquency ten years later—made the following statement:

> Men and women today are conscious more than ever before of problems which face youth during the present war emergency. These problems are not merely matters of local concern, belonging to some township or city, but are nationwide in their scope. And by virtue of the fact that they are nationwide they should receive the intelligent concern of every person in this community.
>
> The problems which have presented themselves will not be solved by any committee or any isolated group. They will be solved by the cooperation of the home, the church, the school, the town government and other agencies, which are cooperating in the building of good citizenship. We must have a unified front.[10]

In another case that would also resurface in 1953, the council pointed out an old axiomatic that idle hands make mischief. They called for a creation of recreation and social programs for youth of all ages, whose purpose would be to "use the leisure hours of the young people so constructively that they will not have either the desire or the time to become involved with malicious mischief."[11]

Nearly a decade passed before attention was once again drawn to the so-called juvenile delinquency problem in Denville. While there were numerous crimes reported between 1945 and 1953—most dealing with theft, abuse and arson—when and if found, the perpetrators were adults. That is until 1952. In the following year, the *Denville Herald* ran an editorial about delinquency issues in the town. It was the first such editorial in ten years, when the town nervously looked for answers to what was happening with its youngest citizens. In a déjà vu moment, the only thing that changed was the fact that the culprits were now ten years older.

The first case to grace the front page of the local paper pertaining to teenage crime made a comeback in January 1952, when it was reported that "Police Nabbed Two Boys on Theft Charge." The two schoolboys, aged fifteen and sixteen, were rounded up by the Denville police chief Harry Jenkins and were charged with breaking, entering and larceny in four unoccupied cabins in the town's Cedar Lake neighborhood. Jenkins said the robberies started on December 21, 1951, with the boys taking the stolen goods to a shack built in the woods north of the lake.[12] The young men, having stolen an air pistol from one of the cabins, proceeded on a spree of shooting windows and lights throughout the area. Furthermore, the chief said, after taking liquor from a cabin, the boys celebrated New Year's Eve by throwing a party for their friends. The two were caught when the police chief found a pencil with the name of the owner of one of the looted cabins on it when searching the shack in the woods for evidence. Pending a hearing from Denville's magistrate, Frank Headley, the boys were released in the custody of their parents.

By the summer of 1952, reports had surfaced of youths vandalizing the Main Street School by throwing bricks through windows and causing hundreds of dollars of damage. That same month, two thefts were reported involving youths at the Arrow Diner and the Sunoco Gas Station, both on Route 6 in Denville. A total exceeding $200 was stolen. Toward the end of September, three more local youths were captured by state troopers after leading the police on a car chase down Route 6 in a vehicle they stole from Bergen Street in Dover.[13] The Denville youngsters crashed the car and

Denville's Broadway—the main town center around the time of the murder. *Denville Historical Society.*

attempted to escape through the woods, where they were apprehended. The driver, being eighteen years old, was fined $50 and sentenced to thirty days in the Morris County Jail, while his accomplices were minors and were once again released in the custody of their parents.[14]

The year 1953 began the same way that 1952 ended, with more reports of juvenile crimes committed by Denville youths. As early as the first week of January, Herbert Terry, the proprietor of Terry's Pharmacy on Broadway, announced that he was $400 poorer after a break-in. Terry stated that $60 of the stolen money was in the cash register and the rest in a cash tin under the register, where he had put it to prepare to make a bank deposit. The *Herald* reported, "It is believed to be the work of juveniles as other valuables such as narcotics, cigarettes, and a camera were not touched, where as great numbers of small coins were included in the haul, the spending of which would be a give-away clue to alert police officers or shop owners."[15] The month of March saw yet another crime, where two local boys and one from Boonton pleaded guilty to larceny charges in a special court session in Denville's Municipal Building. One of the young men was Edwin D., eighteen years old, of Denville, who would play a role in the infamous case few months later.

Edwin and his coconspirators were in the Denville Court to sign confessions to a series of thefts in Denville, Montville, Parsippany, Rutherford, Rockaway and Boonton that had begun two months before. According to the *Denville Herold*, "Three weeks ago [Edwin] and [Irving] took a small trailer from the rear yard of the Hillview Tavern of Rt. 46. Shortly following, they removed 500 pounds of scrap iron from the Rockaway Sales Co. yard and returned several days later for an additional 300 pounds. Two weeks ago, the pair removed an automobile engine from a barn in Split Rock and also about 200 pounds of scrap from a junk yard in Boonton. [Together with the young man from Boonton], all three combined their talents in taking a load of scrap iron from the rear of Peer's store on Diamond Spring Road [today's La Cucina Restaurant]."[16] The thefts of scrap iron, which the young men then promptly sold, continued for another two weeks. Local Denville people and businesses were especially affected, with thefts being reported at Gearhart's used car lot and the Lash property on Kitchell Road. The men were fined and put on probation by the court.

The events of a year prior to the murder of the summer of 1953 prompted the *Denville Herald*'s editor, for the first time in a decade, to publicly acknowledge that the small town might have a juvenile problem:

> *Suppose you read in the paper one morning that 8,167 boys between 13 and 18 had been picked up by the New York City Police in less than two weeks for larceny and other assorted offenses. You no doubt would feel that something was wrong somewhere; with people in general, with the New York judicial system, or with the paper's Linotype operator. And in New York a howl would be set up that could be heard in Rockaway.*
>
> *The story is not all that far-fetched. When it is rewritten in digest style, in pocket-book format and dropped on you own doorstep, we get the same harsh facts....Seven boys in that age group, the same portion or percentage as the 8,167 represents in New York, have confessed to larceny charges in the Denville court in less than two weeks.* [Denville at the time had a population of nearly 6,000 people and was in its biggest population boom.]
>
> *When something may be either socially desirable or harmful, depending on how it is used, society generally tries to prevent the abuses by setting up some kind of license restriction. Those individuals who fail to recognize their obligations are presently deprived of privilege, as in a case of operating an automobile, shooting a gun, or running a tavern. Since parenthood, though necessary to society, is also subject to abuse, there might be some grounds for arguing that it too ought to be licensed.*[17]

In the following week's editorial, the author revealed a conversation he had with "some young fellows" who happened to be "discussing last week's editorial about the amount of juvenile delinquency in Denville." One of the boys summed up his feelings with a question: "Why don't they [the

Aerial view of the town center as it appeared around the time of the murder. *Denville Historical Society.*

community members] give us something to do then?" The editor admitted that it took some questioning on the part of another older youth to make the particular youth admit that he was not justified in causing trouble, "whether the community provided him with year-round entertainment or not."[18] It was as if Denville was having a bad dream. But no one suspected that within a mere four months, it would become a nightmare.

THESE SEEMINGLY UNRELATED EVENTS beginning ten years before the Denville 13 murder expose an interesting correlation, if not necessarily a causation. Namely, the ages of the perpetrators in Denville's first recorded spike in juvenile delinquency would be consistent with the ages of the second—and now teenage—juvenile delinquency issue of the 1950s. In a sense, the youth issues that the town had in the early 1950s did not come from different kids and different problems but from the same generation of youth who simply grew up to became teenagers. Thus, the terrible crime of 1953 can be viewed as a culmination of small-town juvenile delinquency going unchecked for too long. As such, a bigger argument can be made that the man killed on that night in August 1953 was another casualty of World War II. While this is definitely a factor that cannot be ignored, this research will show that there was a multitude of other considerations and circumstances that might have led to thirteen Denville boys committing what could be described as the town's crime of the century.

It would be unfair to cast aspersions on the entire generation of youth because of the actions of a few. As an old proverb states, there's bad apples in whatever way you want to group people—the big mistake is generalizing. Concurrently, as spoken by Philip Zimbardo, an American psychologist known for the 1971 Stanford experiment, sometimes when you put good apples into a bad situation, you will get bad apples.[19] The following story might be the epitome of both.

SUMMER OF 1953

T he summer of 1953 was a very hot one in Denville. Popularly known as the "Hub of Morris County," the town was described in the first book chronicling its history—interestingly enough written around the time of the murders—as "one of New Jersey's better-known smaller communities of year-round and vacation residents."[20] The 1953 boundaries of Denville Township formed a triangle, the southern extremity being the junction of four townships—Denville, Randolph, Parsippany-Troy Hills and Morris—with Mendham Township's northeast corner less than a mile distant. Westerly it was bordered by Rockaway Borough and Rockaway Township and northeasterly by Boonton Township and Mountain Lakes.

As the summer of 1953 was coming to a close, the small town was celebrating the successful implementation of a new Little League Baseball program, the creation and opening of a new St. Claire's Hospital and the long-awaited opening of the new Morris Hills Regional High School—the first of its kind in Morris County. Kids and adults spent their summer nights at the popular restaurant Denville Shack (today's Burger King Restaurant on Route 46), which was a massive crowd pleaser. A town historian of the 1950s through the 1980s, Charles M. toeLaer, described the Shack owner's ability to attract the crowds. At the time, the owner's wife was known to maintain order and dignity. It was reported that she tolerated no horseplay, thus fathers had no concern when their daughters were going to the Shack. Many a man who acted up found himself being dragged out by the ear by the old lady.[21]

The Denville Shack. A popular hangout spot for teens and adults in the 1950s. *Denville Historical Society.*

St. Claire's Hospital opened its doors a month before the lover's lane murder and was still reported on during the week following it. *Denville Historical Society.*

Just like many summers before, people visited the area from all over the county and the state to enjoy the numerous lakeshore beaches the town had to offer. They also came to be entertained, to golf at the town's two ranges, Rockaway Country Club and the Stickle Golf Driving Range, across from the Denville Shack. There was also the movie theater in the center of town on Denville's Broadway Avenue, which showed first-run motion pictures. Vito Bianco, Denville's historian and the author of two books about the history of the town, perhaps summarizes it best when he says, "Denville was not a place where great things happened—just everyday things. It was not a place where the rich and powerful lived—just ordinary people."[22] Yet as many young people went to bed on Sunday, August 30, 1953, anxiously and excitedly awaiting the start of a new school year—some in a brand-new high school—there were others, the same age as them, spending their last night of summer doing something far from sleeping.

The following story has been pieced together from the thirteen suspects' police statements, obtained by the Morris County Prosecutor's Office, as well as numerous in- and out-of-state newspapers and reports on the crime from the time of its occurrence. It is all in the public domain. This is what we know.

SUNDAY, AUGUST 30, 1953, 2:30 A.M.

Paul's Diner, Mountain Lakes

A group of boys, ranging in age between fourteen and twenty-two, were seen sitting in Paul's Diner in Mountain Lakes in the early morning hours. It was a few hours past midnight on Sunday, August 30, 1953. It was a hot summer, as newspapers reported record heat continuing into the nineties for the following week. The summer break was almost over, and one could mistake them for simply spending the last of their careless summer nights hanging out before the drudgery of school beckoned. But that was not the case.

The boys looked out of breath; they were agitated and eyed everyone with suspicion. They spoke in low voices and continued to glance around them to see if anyone was questioning their presence at the diner. Maybe it was because it was so late, and they seemed so out of place. Or maybe because they were afraid of what their parents might say to them when they walked into their living rooms after being out all night. But perhaps it was something else.

Mountain Lakes Diner when it was constructed in the late 1940s. This is what it looked like when the boys spent the night of the murder there. *Denville Historical Society.*

The boys could no longer take the pressure of being watched by other late-night patrons, and after finishing their drinks and not ordering any meals, they hastily left and went their separate ways. Some only went as far as the backseat of their cars parked around the corner, where they spent the last few hours of darkness sleeping off an eventful night. In fact, they left so fast that one of them forgot a wallet, which fell between the cushions of their booth—or was this intentional? And so, in the seat in the diner, a wallet waited to be found—a wallet belonging to the man who, by the end of that day, the young men would all be accused of killing.

SATURDAY, AUGUST 29, 1953, ABOUT 5:00 P.M.

Denville Soda Shoppe, Broadway Avenue

A group of older juveniles, ranging in age between seventeen and twenty-two, met at a local soda shop attached to the town's pharmacy right in the business center. They did not look out of place as they planned out an incident involving a thirty-something-year-old out-of-state male who had rented a local place for the summer and had been hanging around town. It was agreed that the man's obvious wealth and his "preliminary advancements of immoral nature" toward some younger male residents of the town warranted a reprimand. They chose to be the ones to administer it.

Another four boys, some as young as fourteen, were chosen to be the bait for the trap against the man. The plan was to lure him to a lonely spot and

Picture of the Denville Theatre and the Soda Shoppe, where the young men planned the victim's attack. *Denville Historical Society.*

then proceed with other plans of teaching the man a lesson. Extortion was not out of question, as the eldest member of the group at the soda shop told his accomplices that he would bring a camera to try to catch the out-of-state man in "an immoral act...for blackmail purposes." The plan was set, and they left to inform others about the course of events. While only about five of the young men planned the ambush, by the time of the incident, a total of thirteen were involved who knew of it and/or were present during its occurrence.

SATURDAY, AUGUST 29, 1953, ABOUT 6:30 P.M.

Rockaway River Beach, near Savage Road

The four younger boys selected to bait the man arrived at a local beach and hangout spot near the Rockaway River. They were driven there by the man who would become their eventual victim. After picking them up at the soda shop in town, it was he who suggested going for a swim. Unbeknownst to this man, his car was being followed by two other vehicles that had parked off the side of the road. As the man and the four boys piled into his car after swimming at the river, the plan was temporarily derailed. The young men waiting in the cars following the victim noticed that the out-of-state man's car turned right and set off toward Rockway instead of the abandoned Morris Canal towpath that was agreed on by the juveniles as the bait place.

The car with its Virginia license plates seemed out of place in the small town as it made its way to neighboring Rockaway. Also out of place were the two cars that followed closely behind. The car finally came to a stop at Vila Valley Inn, a bar and local hangout spot. Spending money lavishly, the grown man bought beers for the minors as they hung out at the bar. At one point, one of young men snuck out to let his friends outside know that the

Savage Road public beach near the Rockaway River, where the accused met the victim on the night of the murder. *Denville Historical Society.*

The junction of Franklin Road and Route 46, around 1960. The victim likely turned onto the highway heading west toward Rockaway when he was followed by the other young men. *Denville Historical Society.*

man was indeed carrying a lot of money. He also informed them of their next stop—the older man himself suggested the abandoned Morris Canal towpath used by teens as one of the town's lover's lanes. Finally, everything was going according to plan, albeit a bit later than originally planned. It might have been too dark to take pictures of the man's actions, but it was not too late to catch him in the act and teach him a lesson.

As the youth ran back into the bar, the remaining young men waiting in the cars decided to send one of the vehicles to track back to the towpath and wait there in the dark with the lights off. The other car waited in the parking lot of the bar in case there were any last-minute changes in the plan. It was well past midnight as the out-of-state man exited the bar with the four youths. Although they all felt a little buzz from the night of drinking, the older man allowed one of youngsters to drive his car to what he did not yet know would be the last place he would be seen alive.

AUGUST 30, 1953, 1:00 A.M.

Morris Canal Towpath

A local youth taking his girlfriend to the town's lover's lane spot turned onto the lonely towpath only to see the dirt road blocked by the Virginia car, which had just arrived. Upset by their secret spot being occupied, the young sweethearts backed their car out and chose to spend their night somewhere else. The innocent teen's presence created something of a nervous moment for the few boys in the waiting car covered by darkness and the woods at the end of the towpath. They were quickly reassured that not only had the bystander's car left, but they also had not been noticed by the man and the four boys who had just parked. The second car pulled into the towpath's dirt lane with the lights off. The car then blocked the Virginia vehicle from the only possible exit but still kept its distance. It appeared that this car was also not noticed by the out-of-state man or was at least ignored for the time being. Three boys who arrived with the man stepped outside the car as the older male remained inside with one boy. Looking in the car, they saw him "attempting preliminary advances" toward their friend. They signaled to the other cars.

Seemingly out of nowhere or, more specifically, from the darkness on each end of the towpath, a group of boys and young men approached the parked vehicle. The older member of the gang of juveniles looked into the car. One could see the fear on the grown man's face as he was ordered out of his vehicle. With his voice shaking, he refused. The young men did not ask again.

Residents of the new development on George Street woke up to a noise coming from the towpath, which was about thirty-five yards past their street. Albert J. Brantner of 7 George Street sat up in his bed and looked at a wristwatch lying on his nightstand, it was 1:30 a.m. The noise was probably just darn kids again, he thought. It seemed like the densely wooded area near his new house was a "favorite of petters [young lovers]."[23] He decided he would mention this to someone tomorrow, or maybe he would not bother. Tired, Albert lay down and went back to sleep.

⌐───···───⌐

MRS. LILLIAN JONES, BRANTNER'S aunt, who lived in the same house as Albert, noticed a car parked on the towpath around 7:00 a.m. on Sunday morning. Curious, she walked down the path and looked inside the vehicle from one side. Not seeing anything, she went back and asked her nephew to go and take a look. Albert found the blood-spattered body of a man in his early thirties stretched out in a ditch alongside his parked car. Albert promptly reported this to Denville police officer Arthur Stratham.[24] In turn, Police Chief Harry B. Jenkins was notified and immediately called in the county prosecutor's office. The proper authorities were at the scene before 8:00 a.m., and the investigation had begun.

The bludgeoned body lay near his car about six hundred yards off busy Route 46. The face of the body was reported to have been badly cut and bruised and showed that he had been bleeding from the nose and the mouth. County physician William Costello said that death had been caused by a brain hemorrhage resulting from one or more blows to the head.[25] According to the autopsy report obtained from the Morris County Prosecutor's Office, the man had multiple contusions on the left arm, abrasions on the left wrist and chest and lacerations in and around the mouth. There was also evidence of "serour [presumably semen] discharge from his penis."[26] There was no evidence taken

The victim's car as it appeared on the morning of the investigation. *OPRA released file of the Morris County Prosecutor's Office.*

from the body, nor was there any later testimony of those involved that points to the man and the minor having any specific sexual intercourse.

No weapon was found at the scene. The auto beside the body had Virginia license plates with the registration number 347.505. The rear plate had been bent outward so that the number could not be seen.[27]

The thirty-two-year-old victim was identified as Ross E.M., who had been living in the rooming house in the township since the beginning of the summer but formerly resided in Virginia. According to the *Morristown Daily Record*, his body was lying on his back beside the car with his head toward the rear of the vehicle. His face was badly cut and bruised. He was wearing summer shoes and gray slacks, the pockets of which were empty and inside out. The contents of the glove compartment of the car were reported to be scattered about the floor and the front seat of the car. There were also two cameras in the vehicle, which seemed to have been untouched.[28] Another newspaper from out of state reported that in the car were identification papers and a telegram addressed to Lieutenant Ross E.M. Police were unable to explain the military designation.[29]

The Denville Police Department, taken 1954, one year after the murder. Chief Jenkins (*left*) and officer Stratham (*third from the left*) both oversaw the investigation. *Denville Historical Society.*

The body was moved to the Tuttle and Kerner Funeral Home in Rockaway to be held, pending the notification of Ross E.M.'s family. While no relatives had been located in the first twenty-four hours, within days, his family had read about the incident in their local newspapers in North Carolina and thought it might be their son and decided to come to Denville to have their worst fears realized.

The investigation that started promptly at the arrival on the scene was conducted by Chief Harry B. Jenkins of the Denville Township Police and Captain Edward Gebhardt and Detective Edward Burke of the prosecutor's office. Both Prosecutor John D. Collins and Assistant Prosecutor Oscar W. Laurie had also been assigned to the case.[30] Assisted in the apprehension of the suspects by a local citizen who reported seeing the gang with Ross E.M. earlier in the evening, the police completed their arrests by Sunday night, less than twenty-four hours from the time of the incident. Working throughout the day and into the early hours of the next morning yielded more than a dozen suspects. It took an additional few days for the police authorities to complete fifty-two hours of questioning of the total of thirteen suspects who were picked up at the scene.[31] Like a puzzle, pieces soon began to fall into place, and a story was put together.

⌐—···—⌐

Ross E.M.'s BODY WAS identified by Reverend Samuel Coughey of the Pentecostal church in nearby Rockaway. Reportedly, the reverend confirmed that the victim had lived in the area ten years before but returned in June and had been staying in a rooming house.[32] According to his World War II draft card, Ross resided on Main Street in Rockaway, New Jersey, in 1941, where he was a twenty-year-old student at the Eastern Bible Institute in Greenlane, Pennsylvania.[33] The newspaper further reported the questioning of Ross E.M.'s alleged fiancée, Marie H. of Valley Road, Montclair. The report indicated that Ross had worked in a Boonton plastics molding plant when he returned to New Jersey. According to the fiancée, the man had also, just a week before, moved out of Denville and into Boonton. His identification indicated that his permanent address was in Portsmouth, Virginia.[34]

According to his sister-in-law, Mrs. James B.S. of Norfolk, Virginia, the thirty-two-year-old was a member of a locally famous family in North Carolina. His father was a retired member of the military, and nearly all men in the family tree were members of the same branch.[35] By the third day of the investigation, newspapers began to report on the victim's questionable past. Specifically, Ross E.M. had been accused and found guilty of "impairing and debauching the morals of a minor" boy, making him a convicted sex offender.[36] Another newspaper reported that the incident, or incidents, had occurred in 1947 in New Jersey and involved numerous boys.[37] Ross served out his sentence in Rahway State Prison, a maximum-security prison operated by the New Jersey Department of Corrections in Woodbridge Township, New Jersey, from 1947 to 1950.[38] At the time of his incarceration, the prison was overcrowded with prisoners, ranging from rapists to murderers. It also lived up to its maximum-security designation, as early in the 1970s, the *New York Times* reported that it had a lengthy history of grievances of mistreatment by the guards and violent inmates. In fact, shortly after Ross's sentence ended, about 230 prisoners seized a two-story dormitory, holding nine guards as hostages.[39] It is impossible to know how his stay at the infamous prison effected Ross E.M. What can be deduced based on the alleged events of 1953 is that he was not reformed by the institution.

"A SORDID TALE INVOLVING robbery, extortion and morals which resulted in the brutal murder of Ross E.M. 32, in lover's lane of Denville Township early Sunday morning, was unraveled by Assistant Prosecutor Oscar W. Laurie late last night," proclaimed the headline from Thursday, September 3, 1953. At the same time, "Laurie said all 13 of the suspects who have been questioned for the past four days will be charged with murder."[40] That Thursday afternoon, the following boys and young men appeared in the Denville Municipal Court before Magistrate Frank A. Headley for arraignment on charges of murder: George C., twenty-two, of Denville; Richard M., sixteen, of Denville; Jerre H., twenty, of Morris Plains; two brothers, Philip K., nineteen, and John K., fifteen, both of Denville; Edwin D., nineteen, of Denville; Russell C., fourteen, of Denville; Burl C., fifteen, of Denville; Edwin R., fifteen, of Denville; William W., seventeen, of Denville; Donald F., seventeen, of Denville; Lars O., fourteen, of Denville; and Richard K., seventeen, of Rainbow Lakes.[41] The arraignment was scheduled for the afternoon after transportation arrangements were made for the boys and young men, "four of whom were transferred Tuesday to the [juvenile institution] Hudson County Parental Home in Bayonne [New Jersey]."[42]

The police concluded that while some of the thirteen took an active part in the beating of the man, which ultimately resulted in his death, all involved had knowledge of the intent and aided and/or abetted in the eventual beating. Prior to Thursday's arraignment, the press was notified of the assistant prosecutor's investigation and conclusion that there were three motives for the crime: "First, the man was allegedly a homosexual and the group intended to beat him because of it; second, there was intent of robbery; and third, there was apparently an intent of extortion."[43]

Another news outlet reported that the gang of kids "had taken some money, not much, police say, and some papers from [the victim's] wallet."[44] Furthermore, the same source noted that after the young men drove away and met at the diner, the papers were promptly flushed down the drain, the victim's wristwatch was hidden and the wallet was left behind.

The investigation also uncovered that the gang's car was spotted at the scene on Sunday as some attempted to return to the scene of the crime in the early hours of the morning. When they realized that the body had been discovered (seeing Albert J. Brantner and some locals who had gathered as they waited for the police), the youths drove past the scene.[45] The *Philadelphia Inquirer* reported that the police pointed out that the murder might not have been the intent, as "underbrush had been stuffed into the exhaust pipe of [the victim's] auto in an attempt to disguise the slaying."[46] Furthermore, there was information that led the police to believe that "Ross E.M. was not dead when the group fled" but "was apparently in bad shape and the group must have known that because some failed to return home that night."[47]

Police said that when Ross E.M. refused to get out of the car, he was struck on the head with a soda pop bottle, dragged out semiconscious and beaten to (eventual) death.[48] The statements of the accused also revealed that only a few had conceived of the plan, while all others knew of it and agreed to carry it out. By October, the ringleader was identified as George C., who, at twenty-two years old, was the oldest member of the group. It was reported earlier that "George C. [previously] served a prison term in the Annondale State Reformatory on a morals charge with another young man from the group, Edwin D. [being at the time of the crime] on probation after receiving a suspended sentence to Annondale for larceny of a trailer."[49] A search for George C's specific morals charge did not yield any results, but as a morals charge was then defined by the U.S. Department of Justice as "a conduct that shocks the public conscience," one can gain a decent idea of the type of crime it might have been.[50]

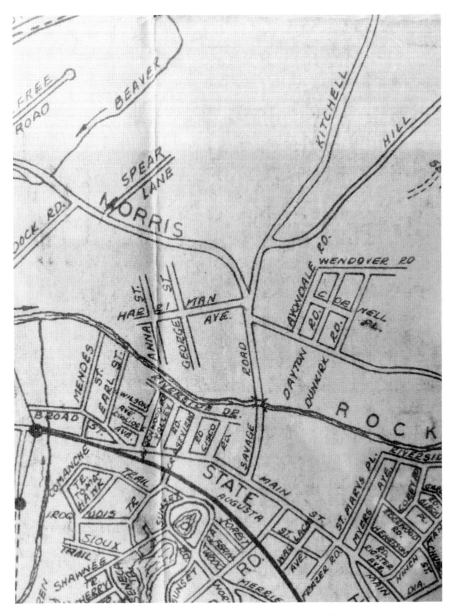

Notice George Street in the center of the map clipping from 1950. The end of this street was where the wooded area of the old canal towpath was used as a lover's lane. *Denville Historical Society.*

As reported on Friday, September 4, 1953, the day after the arraignment, the boys and young men were brought in four cars to the Denville Firehouse for the formal arraignment on Thursday afternoon.[51] Aside from those boys who were kept at a juvenile center, all others had spent the past few days being held in the Morris County Jail. A large group of youngsters, presumably friends of those accused, gathered outside the firehouse with other groups of citizens who remained cautiously across the street.[52] The entire scene was described as very somber and eerily quiet. It was noted that while the magistrate's court usually held meetings on the first floor, due to the large number of accused, the court had to be moved upstairs to a larger room. The old firehouse building stood in the same spot where a new one now stands near Firemen's Field and across the street from the shopping center.

At first, the sullen and drab attitude witnessed outside the firehouse seemed to have transitioned inside the courtroom, with the group of boys appearing morose and calm. This all changed when the mother of the fourteen-year-old Russell C. "threw her arms around him and burst into tears," which accordingly led to tears from others present.[53] Denville chief of police Jenkins read the charges stating that the thirteen young men and boys had "willfully, feloniously, and with malice aforethought kill[ed] and murder[ed] Ross E. M." The defendants all waived a hearing and entered mandatory pleas of not guilty.[54] All but four of the accused were represented by counsel

The "old" Denville Firehouse, where the boys' arraignment took place on the second floor. The sidewalk was full of schoolchildren trying to get a glimpse of their peers entering and exiting the court. *Denville Historical Society.*

Shying away from the camera while arriving for the Denville Township's Magistrate's Court. *From* Denville Herald, *January 15, 1952.*

in the official arraignment. "Edward Broderick of Morristown represented Jerre H., Edwin D., Richard K., Phillip K., [while] Louis Winer also of Morristown, represented Richard M., Edwin R. and George C."[55] The entire event did not take long. After Magistrate Headley explained the reasoning for the hearing to the accused, all the defendants were handcuffed, "nine in groups of three each and four, including the 14-year-old…handcuffed to a chain in a separate group" and escorted out of the building to a still-awaiting crowd of youngsters.[56] The defendants looked embarrassed, with many shielding their faces. In some instances, their parents walked near them to comfort them as they were packed into police vehicles and driven back to the county jail to await the grand jury trial at the county court.

Five weeks had passed as the town and its citizens—still in shock—awaited the decision of the Morris County grand jury. The town newspapers moved on, concentrating on a successful start to a new school year; various new town events, such as little league games; and advertisements for sales at various businesses. When the news broke on October 17, 1953, that Morris County had indicted the thirteen youths on charges of murder, the two highest-selling newspapers in town, the *Denville Herald* and the *Citizen*, did not even run the story. John A Spargo, foreman of the September term of the Morris County grand jury, released a statement condemning the immoral and illegal actions of the nation's youth. The letter was sent to all local police authorities in

Morris County. Judge Waesche thanked the jurors and suggested that their statement blaming lack of moral and spiritual guidance from parents, low church attendance and shortage of organized extracurricular activities should also be sent to "all mayors as head of governing bodies of their respective communities, who have the responsibility to finding means of recreation for the youth."[57]

News of a major turn in the case broke nearly a month later. In the November 10, 1953 edition, the *New York Times* ran a story announcing that the thirteen Denville youths accused of murder would, after all, not go to trial. This time, the news did make the *Denville Herald* and even appeared on the front page. This was the first time anything about the murder was directly covered or mentioned by the town's newspaper since the news broke the day after the actual event, all the way back in the September 3 issue. The *New York Times* reported, "The Superior Court Judge Donald Waesche allowed some of [the accused] to plead guilty to lesser charges [and] ordered others turned over to juvenile authorities for further actions."[58] Concurrently, "the retraction of earlier mandatory pleas of innocent to charges of murder was allowed after consultation between the county prosecutor's office and attorneys for the defendants."[59]

According to the *Denville Herald*, "George C., 22…pleaded guilty to second degree murder; Richard M. 16…Edwin D., 19…and Jerre H., pleaded guilty to manslaughter and all four pleas were accepted."[60] Their sentencing was

Arriving for the Denville Township's Magistrate's Court arraignment for the murder in lover's lane. *From* Morristown Daily Record, *September 4, 1953.*

scheduled for November 20, 1953, ten days after their pleas were changed and entered. For those ten days, George C. and his friends spent their time in county jail contemplating the potential maximum prison terms of thirty years and ten years, respectively. Pleas of guilty to a conspiracy to commit atrocious assault and battery were "entered by Philip K., 19, and John K., 15, Donald F., 17, and Richard K., 17," with the pleas of manslaughter not accepted and referred to juvenile court for "Russell C., 14, Burl C., 15, William W., 17, Edwin, R., 15, and Lars O., 14."[61]

The third and last time the *Denville Herald* mentioned the infamous case that shook the small town was on November 26, 1953, with a headline neatly tucked into the bottom corner of the front page: "Murder Case Disposed of Last Friday."[62] In barely two paragraphs, the town of Denville put the murder behind it once and for all.

The front page of the *Denville Herald* one week after the event. While the *Morristown Daily Record* ran a front-page story each day for a week, the town's newspaper chose to ignore it. *From* Denville Herald, *September 10, 1953.*

According to Paterson's *The News*, from the same week, "George C....whom the police tapped as the ringleader, drew the lone prison sentence imposed by the Superior court Judge Donald Waesche in the case."[63] He received seven to ten years in prison to be served in Bordertown Reformatory on pleading guilty to non vult (no defense) to second-degree murder. All others, including those sentenced on manslaughter charges and the lone charge of conspiring to commit atrocious assault and battery, received suspended sentences and were placed on probation for up to five years.[64] The remaining boys who were referred to juvenile court were also placed on probation. So, all but one came back home to Denville, a town that they were responsible for putting in the national spotlight for the past three months. Life would go on for the Denville 13, as they were dubbed by the newspapers. For at least eleven of them who came back to live in Denville that December 1953, it would not be the same town they were taken away from those few months before. But to be fair, neither would their lives. As with everything that we think we know, there is always more to the story than what the papers are willing—or in this case, not willing—to share.

3
THE TRUTH

T he following is transcribed from the defendants' pleas as they were entered to the Superior Court of New Jersey before Honorable Donald M. Waesche on November 9, 1953, in Morristown, New Jersey. If anything, it proves what we could already deduce for ourselves, namely, that the story of the Denville 13 is a cautionary tale of how one mistake can lead to a life of consequence—how one misjudged situation, as small as getting in a car against one's better judgment or hanging out with people who deep down one knows you should not be around, could put you in a situation from which there is no escape. Assistant Prosecutor Oscar F. Laurie probably summed it up best when describing the unfortunate situation of one of the defendants: "This particular defendant merely went along for the ride," he said, "and it turned out to be a much harder ride than he thought it was going to be."

So, what really happened that night? Who was responsible? What is it exactly that the people of Denville think they secretly know? Until now, there were just rumors, some exaggerated and some whitewashed. For the first time in seventy years, the evidence and notes from the Morris County Prosecutor's Office have been released and reviewed. We get a little more insight into what exactly transpired that night. All of the quoted material appears directly as spoken in court on that day, according to court transcripts filed in Morristown, unless otherwise noted by brackets.

THE COURTHOUSE IN MORRISTOWN seemed a bit cold. It was Monday, November 9, 1953. Edwin R. shifted in his seat; he was sitting along with his so-called coconspirators. He missed his parents. It was later stated in front of the same court that Edwin was one of the youngest teens who lured Ross E.M. to lover's lane. Why did he get into that man's car, he thought to himself? He could still remember sitting in the back seat with Burl C. and Russell C., trying to see past the tall William W., who, even while sitting behind the wheel of the Virginia car, seemed the biggest and oldest of the four boys. It no longer mattered that he did not partake in any of the beatings and stayed to the side when he got out of the car to leave Russell in there with the grown man. Edwin woke up from the daze just in time to hear the prosecutor making his case in front of the judge. "In view of the fact that he assisted in luring this victim to this unfortunate assault, I would like to note for the record that I enter a plea of guilty of manslaughter."

The attorney for Edwin interjected, "The tragic thing, Your Honor, is that this young man is 16 years old today. At the time of the commission of this offense, he was 15." It would be one birthday he would want to forget.

The judge noted his plea of manslaughter and referred his case to juvenile court. Edwin put his head down and watched his friend William W. receive the same verdict for the same reasons. Introduced to the court as one of the boys who lured the victim to the lonely spot, William's case was only different in that he was the one driving the car and had "put it in the spot where it had been put at the time the crime was committed." He was, however, also a bystander, according to the prosecution. These two verdicts and referrals to juvenile court were consistent with another decision regarding yet another young boy who was a passenger in the victim's car.

According to Burl C.'s attorney, he was presumably the most aloof of the boys in Ross E.M.'s car: "I think the records will show, and the State's evidence will show, that young [Burl] had nothing to do with the striking or with the planning, but went along with the crowd who were going to beat up the victim." The defense added, "I think the records will also show, through the Probation Office report, that this boy, when fully informed, he was like the girl in the Old Country Store who could not say no; and that is the trouble with this boy. Because of that, he has a previous record of arson, where he went into a house with Russel C." It was also brought up that it was Burl that was initially singled out by the ringleaders to act as "the lure for this particular victim to get him in this lonely spot where he was beaten up and eventually died."

Toward the end of the bench sat four boys who really could not believe they had found themselves in this company. Philip knew that, as the older brother, he never should have let his brother John get involved with this group. He never should have asked him to come that night. But then again, he was not supposed to be there himself. When one of the eventual thirteen asked him that night if he wanted to go for a ride to chase this man out of town, he did not think he had anything better to do. It was, unfortunately, also one of the only times he let his younger brother accompany him anywhere.

"May it please the Court, Philip K. is 19 years of age; but our investigation, and I think the investigation of the State, will show that he took no part in planning this thing, he took no part in the assault, he took no part in the robbery. Very unfortunately, he was [only] aware that this group of young men intended to run this man out of town. He went along with them. He did not participate in it [yet] he did not do anything to stop it." The attorney added that, according to the testimonies, Philip, as well as his younger brother, John, stood way off to the side, away from the violent proceedings near the victim's car. Both brothers entered pleas of guilty to conspiracy to commit atrocious assault and battery. The prosecutor summarized their case as two boys who "merely went along for the ride," one that did not turn out the way they could ever envision.

Sitting next to Phillip and John was another fourteen-year-old boy. Donald F. could not get it out of his head—why did he even go to the movies that night? If only he had stayed home like his parents wanted him to. He still remembered running. Every night in jail, he still dreamt of running—running as fast as he could away from what quickly turned out to be something he did not sign up for, running for home where his parents slept in their beds, running to tell them what had happened.

"May it please the Court, at this time I would like to file a retraxit to the previous plea of not guilty to murder and enter a plea of guilty to conspiracy to commit atrocious assault and battery; and ask this case be referred to the Juvenile Court, because Donald is 17 years of age."

As the judge looked down on his notes, the defense continued, "I might say, with the Court's permission, that [Donald] had absolutely nothing to do with the planning, he knew nothing about it. Unfortunately, that evening he went to the movies and he was walking home and was in the vicinity of where this took place, when he met one of the boys, and asked what they were doing. They said they had 'a queer and were going to beat him up.' So, he went along for the ride."

Denville Movie Theatre, a popular attraction for young teens. One of the suspects flagged down a ride home from the rest of the suspects here. *Denville Historical Society.*

The judge motioned for the attorney to continue. "He did not participate in the planning, [or] the robbery; in fact, when the beating started, he ran home from the beating after one or two of the blows had been struck. Unfortunately, he is a victim of circumstance. He went for the thrill but I think the State will agree he knew nothing [about it] except the fact that they had a person of peculiar sexual tendencies in the vicinity and they were going to run him out of the community."

Donald sat in the pew with his head down. The silence from the court was nerve racking to say the least. He heard the prosecutor begin speaking, "Your Honor, I think that [Donald's attorney] has stated pretty much what the State could prove against this defendant."

The prosecutor continued, "I might say further that the State has a witness, an eye-witness, totally impartial in this case, who verifies that fact he saw one of the boys—and we assume it was [Donald], because no one else claims to have left beforehand other than [him]—and this other eye-witness saw him leaving before the rest left the scene." After a brief pause, he continued, "So the State feels that unquestionably [Donald] did certainly at least not have the intent at the time the beating was going on, and tried to get out of there so he would not be a participant in the matter." The prosecutor's statement had a positive effect, as the suggestion to change the plea to guilty of conspiracy was promptly granted. The case, like many of the others, was referred to juvenile court for sentencing.

The last boy sitting with Philip K., John K. and Donald F. was seventeen-year-old Richard K. "He is practically, Your Honor, in the same classification and category as the two [brothers], who just preceded," began the young man's defense. "He took no part in the planning of it, he took no part in the assault, he took no part in the robbery. He, unfortunately, joined with these boys to drive this man out of town. He was [simply] present and did nothing to stop them."

Seeing a pattern here, the judge turned to the prosecutor, asking, "This defendant took no part?"

"No, Your Honor."

"Because this defendant took no part in the planning and took no part in the assault and battery, nor in the robbery," the judge paused to review his notes. "Did he?"

"No," answered the prosecutor. "He did not even know a robbery was to be committed. His position, I might say, was in the back of the car when the beating was taking place. He [stayed in the car and] was in the area, but not even close by." This seemed to satisfy the judge, who proceeded to note the plea of guilty to conspiracy to commit atrocious assault but, like with the others, referred the case to juvenile court.

Jerry H., Lars O. and Edwin D. knew deep down that it would not be them who would take center stage that day. Like the boys whose cases had already been heard by the court, they knew that while they might have played bigger roles in what transpired that night, they were by no means the main culprits. That honor would be left to George C., Russell C. and Richard M.

After the attorney for Jerry H. entered the plea of guilty to manslaughter, the prosecutor began to state his case with the fact that the twenty-year-old did not know the victim was going to be robbed, but "in fact, did, in his own statement admit to the fact that he went through the victim's pockets after the victim was beaten and was lying there on the ground unconscious." What made the case a bit more complicated was what the prosecutor revealed after.

Jerry knew he was in trouble—he knew it that night. Things had gotten out of hand. They were just supposed to drive this guy out of town and scare him a bit. Jerry remembered being told to go through the grown man's pockets as he was lying there. He did not remember why he obeyed or who told him to do so. There was so much blood. Three dollars—that was the amount of money that made him take an active part in the eventual death of Ross E.M. Three dollars. Just a few minutes before, he was trying to stop Richard M. from beating the victim and getting hit in the process. He couldn't stop George C., but at least he stopped Richard. But it was too late—the man was unconscious. Jerry's heart rate was up; he was shaking and then someone said, "Jerry check his pockets."

It was now up to the prosecutor to present his case. "He did participate in robbing the victim, but because of the fact that he attempted to stop the beating that was being inflicted upon the victim—in fact, did prevent [Richard M.], from [Richard M.]'s own statement and from the statements of others, from hitting the victim any longer and tried to do what he could at the time to aid the victim....I recommend that the plea of guilty to manslaughter by this defendant be...accepted."

The judge was not going to make this easy. "Is there any previous record against this defendant?

"No, Your Honor. This defendant has no previous record. I might say he has a good reputation, and he just recently came out of Service. His reputation in the communities wherein he has resided is good."

"This defendant did not take part in the actual striking of the deceased, did he?"

"No, Sir. In fact, he attempted [and succeeded] to stop it, which I think—" The prosecutor was cut off by the judge.

"He did attempt to?"

"Yes, he did, according to a statement of [Richard M.] and himself and statements of other of the accomplices, he did stop [him]."

There was a brief pause. Jerry could not bring himself to look up at the judge. Then the judge continued, "In view of his good reputation and no previous record, I will accept his plea of guilty to manslaughter." The boy exhaled; he did not even realize he was holding his breath.

One of the attorneys stood up to speak again. "[Lars O.] is but 15 years of age, Your Honor...but he was aware of the fact that an effort was being made to run the victim out of the community, and that the primary purpose and motive was assault.

"But because of his age, I would like to enter a plea of guilty to manslaughter and request the Court to refer the matter to Juvenile Court."

The prosecutor concurred with the defense. When prompted by the judge to present his case, he continued, "This defendant, Your Honor, was in this plan from the very beginning; in fact, [he] made an effort, along with Burl C. [who himself was instructed to do so by Russel C.] to have the victim pick him up before they got in the car and went down swimming.

"At the time the assault was committed upon the victim, we have statements to establish the fact that this defendant did take a bottle out of the back of the car, and whether he handed it to George C. or whether George C. took it from him, that we do not know; but we do know that the bottle was taken by him and it got into George's hands; and we believe and we have evidence, from some of the statements, that George C. used the bottle to strike at the victim."

Lars wished he could speak. He hadn't handed George C. that bottle; it was Russel C. who took it from him and handed it to the oldest boy. "May I just make one statement, Your Honor?" interjected Lars's attorney.

"Yes."

"My investigation reveals that the young man was there, but that the bottle was taken from [Russell C.], not from this young man." He doubted that would have made a difference that night or in the courtroom on that day, but at least Lars knew that the truth would prevail and be recorded for posterity. Again, as with the other cases, the plea of manslaughter was recorded but ultimately sent to juvenile court for sentencing.

"I understand that Edwin [D.]'s attorney wishes to enter a new plea of manslaughter," began the prosecutor. "He is 19 years of age and has had a previous criminal record."

"[I should also mention,] he is reputedly a good friend of George C's, and following the commission of the crime he spent many hours with George C. [at the diner that some of the gang had visited after the crime]. He was [also] present when the plan to attack the victim was originally discussed." Edwin D. was not as self-assured as his friend George, who seemed unfazed by the proceedings. In fact, Edwin refused to look up as his case was being discussed. He knew he was there with George at the soda shop when the whole plan was being hatched. He knew he drove the car that followed Ross E.M.'s car and then blocked it in with his, preventing any escape. He knew he spent some of the money taken from the body. And he knew that the prosecutor knew it all as well.

After the prosecutor presented the evidence against the boy and thoroughly explained Edwin's involvement, the case came down to a technicality. As the young man's knowledge of the supposedly intended robbery could not be proven, even though he eventually took and spent some of the victim's money, this, plus the fact that he never struck the victim, excluded him from being tried for murder. The judge motioned to accept the plea of manslaughter. Edwin D. knew he had dodged a bullet. The courtroom's noise level seemed to go up as people began to feel anxious from sitting down for so long.

The judge could sense the restlessness. A short recess was called.

⌐─ ··· ─⌐

As the boys came back into the courtroom, there were only three more cases to be heard, one of which was the oldest member of the group and one the youngest.

George William C. was sitting up straight. There was no fear on his face, if anything, there was indifference. He knew how this worked, having already been tried and found guilty before. Heck, he'd even been to jail before. While others tried not to make eye contact with the judge, George C.'s stare never wavered from looking straight at the magistrate. The real show was about to start.

"I am willing to plead [George C.] to second degree [murder] and throw him on the mercy of the Court for sentence." The attorney for the elder member of the gang did not seem overly enthusiastic in his defense on that day. If anything, his lackluster attitude showed his displeasure in being appointed the young man's lawyer.

The remainder of the boys shifted in their seats. The rumor was that George C. was going to be tried for first-degree murder, and this certainly was a turn of events. The prosecutor began:

> *With respect to this defendant, Your Honor, according to the report by Doctor Collins, who examined the defendant to determine whether he was mentally competent or not, Doctor Collins reports that he is below average in mentality.*
>
> *While it is true that he did not talk to others about robbing the victim, and because of the fact that both he and [Richard M.] struck the victim, and because of the testimonies of his accomplices that say that they saw him slap the victim, and not punch him, the State believes it might have some difficulty proving first degree murder to the satisfaction of the jury.... because...the only intent was to beat up the victim because of alleged sexual perversion, and because many of the same accomplices deny that robbery was motive, the case for first degree murder is not clear.*

The prosecutor went on for a while, describing George C.'s age as the oldest of the group, his mentality and the evidence of him consuming alcohol earlier that evening at a local tavern. In fact, the bartender had described George C. as having drunk a decent number of alcoholic beverages. It was also noted that there were empty beer containers at the scene of the crime that had presumably come from George C.'s vehicle.

Leaving the police station are (*from left to right*) Assistant County Prosecutor Oscar Laurie (who was in charge of the case), Rockway captain Chipko and murder suspect George C. *From* Morristown Daily Record, *August 31, 1953.*

"He has a record of previous offenses, has he not?" asked the judge.

"Yes, Your Honor. He has a record of one previous conviction for debauchery [unrestrained indulgence in sexual activity, drunkenness or drug abuse]," said the prosecutor.

Before the judge began to speak, he seemed to take a while checking his notes again. "Well, there appears to be no evidence that the accused—in fact, it does not appear that any of the defendants—actually intended to kill the deceased.

"That is a correct statement, Your Honor," said the assistant prosecutor.

"Of course, a killing committed in the perpetration of a robbery is murder in the first degree," returned the judge.

The judge met George C.'s gaze. The young man's smug expression said it all. He knew he was getting away with murder, so to speak. He knew, as did the prosecutor and the judge, that robbery was not the real reason for what transpired that night. One could hear the disdain in the judge's voice as he read his verdict, "Since it does not appear that robbery was the real or primary purpose, or that it was the motive for committing atrocious assault and battery from which the deceased died....I will accept the plea to second degree murder.

"The defendant will be remanded to jail to await sentencing." Honorable Donald M. Waesche could have sworn he saw a faint smile on George's face as the verdict was being read.

As Richard M.'s name was called, instead of looking up at the young man, some of the boys' eyes shifted to the diminutive boy sitting quietly among them. Russel C. knew that he would go last on that day. Fitting, perhaps, as some could claim that it was his show all along and thus his encore to give. Richard M., as the only young man besides George C. to have hit the victim, was not in a good position that day, and he knew it. His fears were only further confirmed when the prosecutor tried to discredit his defense: "Undoubtedly, as his attorney, would make every effort to put the entire responsibility on George C."

The prosecutor went on to acknowledge that the use of the bottle in the beating, which likely led to the victim's mortal wounds, was only seen to have been handled by George. As such, he acknowledged that this might confuse the jury about Richard's role in causing Ross E.M.'s eventual death. Just when it seemed that the prosecutor was really going to challenge the defense for the first time that day, he ended with, "As one of the persons who was in charge of this investigation, I felt all along that this defendant, as well as others, was led into this affair by George C." Looking at the accused, who looked up briefly enough to meet the prosecutor's gaze, he continued, "And I do not feel that [Richard M.]'s guilt is as great as George C.'s."

"No previous record?" asked the court. The negative response from the defense seemed enough, as the judge accepted the plea of guilty of manslaughter. Richard M. breathed a sigh of relief.

To a keen eye, it seemed as if Prosecutor Oscar Laurie straightened up just a tad more as he read the next name, Russel C.

After the attorney described the defendant as fourteen years of age and recommended that his plea be entered as guilty of manslaughter, followed by referral to juvenile court for sentencing, the prosecutor concurred, with some reservations.

"This is satisfactory to me, Your Honor. I would like to say something about this particular defendant." Russel felt his face grow red. He felt tears swelling up. But he was not going to cry—not here and not now. The prosecutor continued, "Although this defendant is a mere child, in my opinion and in the opinion of those who investigated this case, he was as much of a ringleader in this group of boys as George William C., and he did almost as much as George did to instigate the commission of this crime.

"However, from the statements which we received from the other accomplices, he apparently—and I say 'apparently' because I don't know—had no knowledge that a robbery was going to be committed." Russel could feel the prosecutor's scrutiny toward him as he listened. "And that he felt all along that the only purpose in the assault which was being committed upon his victim was to beat him up and then chase him out of town." He admitted that the "defendant [had] quite a part in this case," but due to circumstances or motive and the fact that he did not actually strike the victim, the plea of manslaughter would be justified. One could sense that to Prosecutor Laurie, one had gotten away. He did, however, ask the court to hold the boy in county jail until the juvenile court sentencing if the judge would see it as appropriate.

If nobody else sensed the urgency in the prosecutor's delivery, it did not escape Honorable Waesche. "Russel, your offense is a very serious one," the judge began. This time the young boy looked up. "You could be tried here for murder in the first degree. Your part in this was apparently a major part. The fact that you are only 14 years of age would not prevent you being tried here on this serious charge."

"The policy of the law, Russel, is to consider that you did not commit a crime, and that general policy of the law may be considered in deciding whether or not to accept a plea of manslaughter on your behalf. Your plea of manslaughter will be noted on the record, [but] it will not be accepted at this time." The young boy was notified that a probation officer was to be assigned to his case, and based on the officer filing a petition in the juvenile court for his case to be heard there, the indictment against Russel for murder would only then be dismissed and disposed of in said court. Looking at the young boy, the judge reiterated, "I am not accepting his plea at this time."

⌐—··—⌐

BEFORE THE COURT DELIVERED its discourse, it was noted by the prosecution, as well as the defense, that parents of the accused were to be thanked for their cooperation and their instruction to their children to tell the truth. It was noted that in nearly all cases, the parents were present when the statements were taken "and did tell these boys to tell us everything that had taken place." Further thanks were extended to the Denville Police Department, particularly Chief Harry Jenkins, for making it "possible for this case—which could have been a very nasty, complicated, involved case—to be cleaned up as rapidly as it was." The case might have been "cleaned up," but the town's wounds from the event were still very much open.

4
A TOWN TORN APART

SUNDAY, SEPTEMBER 6, 1953, 8:00 P.M.

Denville Community Church, Diamond Spring Road

The following is based on the transcript of the first town hall forum. All quotes are transcribed word for word as they were spoken, unless otherwise noted with brackets.

It felt like a wake. As people entered the church, one could hear murmurs. Friends greeted old friends. Everyone seemed a bit dazed. It had been exactly one week since the body of Ross E.M. was found lying badly beaten next to his car in one of Denville's lover's lanes. Everyone knew why they were the church, yet no one really knew.

Reverend Julius Brashor, who would act as the moderator that night, walked up and down the pews greeting people. Some he knew from Sunday mass. Others he was seeing for the first time. He scanned through the crowds. There must be about forty people here, he thought to himself. There were still more on their way. In the front of the church, by the altar, there was a table set up with chairs and microphones. A group of men and one woman were standing near it, talking as if waiting to be ushered to the seats just directly in front of them. One, clearly a smoker, was fidgeting with a box of matches and seemed to stand a little to the side. All men were dressed in suits and ties, except one taller gentleman who was wearing a police

Denville's United Methodist Community Church as it stood in 1953 during the township panel hearings on juvenile delinquency. The building was eventually destroyed, as the church moved to its new location down Diamond Spring Road. *Denville Historical Society.*

uniform. Harry B. Jenkins, who had, not long ago, taken over as interim chief of police before becoming the town's second official police chief, was not looking forward to this night. The chief looked tired. It had been a long week—the longest of his police career. He knew he would have to face the town. He looked up just at the right time to see Reverend Brashor pointing to his watch. It was 8:00 p.m.—time to start.

Jenkins sat down in a chair between the town's magistrate, Frank Headley, and Jerome Schreiber, president of the Rotary Club of Denville. Sitting at the head of the table on opposite ends were James Whiton, editor of the *Denville Herald*, the apparent smoker, who first broke the news of the crime to the little town, but had since been quiet about the issue, and the only woman on the panel, Ms. Henry Hamilton, the chair of the local juvenile conference committee.

Jenkins looked over at Whiton, whose editorial attacking the town organizations, parents and even a few specific individuals was still the talk of the town. He probably should have addressed it that night. But in the end, he didn't. He was not there to add more fuel to the fire; he was there to extinguish the flame. Reverend Brashor, standing on the side of the table, announced to the crowd still trickling in that this was to be the first of a few scheduled forums on the topic of juvenile delinquency. The day's topic was curfew.

Jenkins worried that he might not have a choice but to confront the editor in public. The opportunity presented itself quite quickly, as Mr. Whiton did not waste time bringing up the most contentious point of his editorial: "I think we need to address the lack of recreational facilities and activities for children in Denville."

Not wanting this to turn into a conversation of the lake communities versus the rest of the town—or even one lake community over another—Ms. Hamilton quickly interjected. "The most delinquent groups in town are not interested in programs where they have to submit to authority." Heads nodded in the audience. "Even such socially desirable agencies in as YMCA and Church groups take points off for youthful misbehavior," which she claimed only turned those types of kids away. Before the conversation could take a nasty turn into a quarrel between Mr. Whiton and Ms. Hamilton, Reverend Brashor interjected, bringing the attention back to the initial topic.

"Is a curfew enforceable?" Brashor asked. Jenkins knew it was his turn—his chance to stand up for the police. He had been hearing enough queries and murmurs about town, questioning the competence of his police force. Yet before he had a chance to speak, Judge Headley interjected. His demeanor was very calm, and his speech was loud and clear, perfected by years as a judicial magistrate.

Denville chief of police Harry B. Jenkins in 1955. *Denville Historical Society.*

"First off, I do not think that instituting a curfew is legal....I am also not impressed with curfews." Prompted to elaborate, the judge continued, "I do not think that curfews are uniformly enforced." Was that meant as a slight? The thought crossed Jenkins's mind, but he let it go; perhaps he was being too defensive, he thought to himself. The magistrate continued, "No law should be a handle to use in individual cases....A curfew would affect the great majority of children who do not get into trouble anyway but would not really curb the small minority who cause trouble." Signaling toward Chief Jenkins, the judge concluded with, "It would also build up resentment against authority."

Jenkins nodded in agreement. Maybe this was not going be a united front against his police force and its presumed failure in allowing the crime to happen in the first place. For the first time that night, he felt reassured that the conversation was not going to go in that direction. "A curfew should originate at home and should be tailored to individual cases then it could perhaps be used as a reward for good behavior," finished the judge.

"Chief Jenkins," began the Reverend, "what is the current state of juvenile delinquency in our town?" Jenkins shifted in his seat. He cleared his throat just loud enough for people to notice that he felt a bit anxious, perhaps even put on the spot. You are here to extinguish fires, he told himself. "Despite the publicity given to the arrest of 13 local youths on a murder charge, there really is not much juvenile delinquency in Denville." For a moment, the room seemed even quieter than the concentrated stillness that had already characterized the mood. Glancing at the public, as if he were speaking directly to them and not the panel, the chief noticed a few heads nodding in approval.

He continued his thought, "Numerically the problem is not serious, but it is extremely serious in a few cases." These were being handled on an individual basis. Before a follow up question was asked, the chief of police pointed to Judge Headley and continued, "[With regard to the curfew], it is not fair to penalize all for the misdeeds of a few; there is also the question on how a curfew would be enforced."

When Jenkins reached for his glass of water, the reverend and moderator for the forum saw it as a sign that the police officer was done talking but instead of moving on, the chief pressed on.

Jenkins placed the glass down on the table. "There is the question of what police should do if they took the child home and found no parents there? Dover's [the town next door] curfew is not enforced, and the Denville police department just hasn't manpower to enforce one." He knew he had to admit to that. "And then there is the problem of children coming out of the movies [in the center of town] after curfew hour." Pointing to the audience, he added, "Some parents would resent interference with what they considered proper activity of their children." The chief witnessed more nods from the crowd.

Seizing the opportunity, Ms. Hamilton added, "No child should be out after 10 p.m. on a school night."

Having been rebuked early on, Mr. Whiton tried to steer the conversation in a new direction, "I do not favor the curfew, which I think is probably a violation of constitutional rights and might even lead to charges of assault against a police officer who compelled a child to go home in a police car when no other law had been broken." Raising his voice just enough to be noticed, the *Denville Herald* editor returned to the earlier point raised by Ms. Hamilton: "The source of the problem is in the home with the parents, it would be better to concentrate on that line."

The reverend saw a perfect opportunity to take a break. As people began to mingle and talk about what was just said, some moved closer to the front. It was almost time for the question-and-answer session—the real test of this forum's ability to stay civil and avoid any finger pointing. Chief Jenkins, having tried to stay out of the public for the past few days as his investigation continued, knew that it was time to face the people. He also knew that this could go either way.

Al Del Pomo, the first one to be selected from the audience, began the questioning: "Is there any legal basis for action against loitering?"

Before Judge Headley had a chance to answer, Chief Jenkins seized his opportunity in the brief pause that followed the question. "There is under the disorderly persons act, but only when it can be proved there is a deliberate intent to interfere with other persons."

As if deliberately cutting him off, Ms. Hamilton asked, "Don't children often taunt the police?"

Would the panel turn against him? Were they going to blame the police for this crime? It would have been the easy thing to do. Jenkins hoped not, but he also knew that there were a lot of factors that made the job of being part of a small-town police force very difficult. The results were certainly imperfect.

"They do [taunt us], especially since the law was changed to raise the juvenile classification from age 16 to age 18. Under the old law the county judge or his prosecutor could refer cases to the local magistrate as a juvenile reference, now all persons under 18 must have their cases handled by the juvenile court in Morristown." He cleared his throat and continued, "The police have had to take a lot of abuse since then...as the juveniles know they cannot be arrested. Many of the boys are big and rugged but we have to handle them as infants."

The reverend prompted him to elaborate.

"'You can't lock me up' is their defiant attitude. I strongly favor returning the law to its previous stand, lowering the juvenile age to 16 and giving discretionary power in handling 16 to 18-year-olds," explained the police chief.

Reverend Brashor looked into the audience of raised hands and selected Lester Heiss of Indian Lake—one of the lake communities under attack by Whiton's editorial in the *Denville Herald*. There was a feeling of anticipation when Mr. Heiss stood up to ask his question. Luckily, the conversation did not veer in the direction of bickering—quite the opposite. "[Could someone explain] why the Dover curfew is still on the books if it is not enforced?" he asked.

Judge Headley wasted no time in answering, "Inertia." Mr. Heiss remained standing, waiting for some form of elaboration. When it became clear that none was forthcoming, he sat back down. Some people stirred in the audience. They came here for answers, and so far, the panel had not really delivered.

Jenkins, feeling that the man deserved a bit more of an explanation, proceeded to address Mr. Heiss, "Times and conditions have changed and 9:30 curfew hour might have seemed good when the rule was adopted many years ago, but is not realistic today."

From that point on, for some reason, Chief Jenkins had the feeling that this was going to be his show. After all, the small town was just thrust into its own murder of a century, and he was the one in charge of solving the case. After making himself the most approachable of the group that made up the panel, Jenkins kept receiving questions directed at him.

Another "laker," John Zieger, from Cedar Lake, was selected to ask his question. "How thoroughly do the police patrol the township's 'hot spots,' such as where the murder was committed?"

There was no hiding from this, and Jenkins knew it. His force was not big enough. "There is one man on night duty, whose job includes checking of the doors of business places, answering phone calls, as well as patrolling the 12 square miles of the Denville's area. It is physically impossible to check the many hidden places effectively." When pressed on the importance of the issue, Jenkins responded, "Police reports do show that [these places] are often visited and many drivers found there are told to move on." It was important to show that this was not neglect. His force was doing the best it could. While preparing for this night and prompted by his own curiosity, the chief had one of his deputies look into the recently conducted 1950 census. The document just reaffirmed what he already knew—the town of Denville was going through a transition from a summer lake community to a full-blown suburban town.

Denville's magistrate, F.H. Headley, who presided over the first arraignment at Denville's Firehouse, on September 4, 1953. *From* Denville Herald, *January 15, 1952.*

2nd Forum to View Schools & Delinquency

Another forum on the juvenile problem in Denville will be held in the Community Church on Sunday at 8 p.m. A panel of local school representatives will discuss the question: "Is our present educational system adequate in regard to problem children?"

Points to be taken up include what the educational system is doing for the problem child, whether extra-curricular activities are over-emphasized, what is the children's attitude toward the school system, the importance of family finances in delinquency, and whether present recreational programs are "giving too much" to our youth.

In charge of arranging this and possibly other forums is a committee consisting of Dr. J. E. Schreiber; Raymond J. Jenny, K. Robert Thompson, Mrs. Frank A. Headley and Mrs. Howard E. Dorer. They will work under the name of the Denville Community Forum.

Announcement of the second town forum, regarding the discussion on juvenile delinquency. *From* the Denville Herald, *September 10, 1953.*

In a mere ten years, from 1940 to 1950, the township's population had more than doubled.[65] The town's building department saw a spike in new home construction permits go from 4 in 1945 to 157 in 1949.[66]

After another person asked about police efficiency, Jenkins brought up his recent findings with those assembled. "Increased population has created heavier police work load and I think that the police department was already at minimum strength [which prompted the hiring of Patrolman Olenowski]," he added, "[Unfortunately], Olenowski was injured last year and is still not able to return to work."

One could hear a side conversation between John Zieger and others near the panel table. Reverend Brashor locked eyes with Mr. Zieger, who was prompted to ask another question. The man stood up once more, asking, "What do the police do about the parents of bad children?"

Jenkins, now firmly in charge of the proceedings, spoke slowly, "The general policy is to try and correct the condition without formal action." Sensing the need for more details, he continued, "This often involves bringing the parents before Judge Headley for questioning and advice. [I think] this has had good results." Headley nodded in agreement. "When a case goes to juvenile court, a first offender is invariably placed on probation in his parents' custody."

When prompted about the success rate of this precedent, Jenkins went on to say, "The parents are granted ample opportunity to meet the problem, but some parents are unwilling or incapable of coping with it."

Headley added, "Parents are then brought before a Juvenile Conference Committee appointed by Judge Barrett."

As the night's event was ending, the panel continued to answer more questions about a possible curfew, when Jenkins admitted that "most serious juvenile offenses happen before 9:30 p.m., so a curfew would not guarantee protection."

Judge Headley also admitted that while the average parent would respect a curfew if it were implemented, "those we want to reach would not." Pushed on the point of being harsher with his punishments, the magistrate went on the defensive, stating, "Many parents [of such kids who get in trouble] cannot pay even a small fine without causing real hardship in the family." He pointed out, "If I put them in jail, I break up a home."

There were also some questions about possible recreational activity programs to keep the kids busy. This was rebuked by Mr. Whiton, who initially brought up the issue at the beginning of the forum. He now seemed to doubt that activities and programs would reach the small percentage of those who needed them most—he meant the fiscally strapped and/or non-lake communities of the town. Jenkins was surprised that it took this long for the editor to speak up. He liked the man and probably even respected him for his bluntness. But he really wanted to keep this meeting civil. So far, the outspoken editor had really let his newspaper be his vessel for sharing his thoughts. The forum seemed to have taken a back seat. Jenkins concurred with Whiton, "I doubt it [that the programs would reach those who need them most]; but I am still in favor of having them. [Of course, we need to acknowledge] that the bad boys oppose supervised activity [which will play a role in them not wanting to be part of these programs in the first place]."

Whiton commented, "Too many programs consist of giving the kids everything on a silver platter with the result that the youngsters do not value the advantages offered." He then added, "Would it be possible to enlist the leadership ability which some of the delinquents obviously possess but turning it into a more desirable activity." Someone in the audience suggested a vocational program or school.

After the idea was dismissed for lack of funds, the floor was given to a township committee man, Page Powell, who solicited a rambunctious response from the crowd when he suggested a "tougher" police policy: "A nightstick applied in the right place."

Judge Headley waved Chief Jenkins off and, with an almost annoyed look, answered, "These are juveniles; if the police lay a hand on them, they can be sued for assault and battery." Since he now had command of the room, he decided to hold on to it for a while longer. "You must [all] remember that we are often dealing with grown-ups, parents, who have no more ability to reason and to manage their affairs wisely than a six or seventh grade child." This only made matters worse, he contended, when trying to keep these juvenile delinquents in check. Charles Laurent, president of the Indian Lake Community Club, concurred with the judge when he got up to speak and commented on "parents who are sure their children are in no trouble, when everyone else knows they are."

Jenkins was tired. It had been nearly two hours of questions and discussion. He knew he had a tough week ahead of him. The case might have been wrapped up, but the repercussions from the crime would continue to define his job in the coming weeks, months or even years. When Howard Dorer got up and asked his question, the chief saw it as perfect opportunity to bring the meeting to a close with a message for the town's citizens. "[Does] the police welcome calls from citizens who think something wrong is going on?" asked the concerned man.

Jenkins chuckled and, with a tired smile, responded, "The police work would be much easier if everyone would report things promptly, even if they seem trivial. Often one incident is linked to another to help solve a much different problem." Before giving the floor back to Reverend Brashor to call the end to the town hall, the chief added, "We aren't psychic. Too many people take the attitude of 'let the police find out for themselves.' We can do a much better job if we get more cooperation."

After leaving the church that night, Chief Harry B. Jenkins got in his police car—one of two that the town owned. He took a deep breath. Was it possible to assign blame? Wasn't the victim in the wrong as well? Is a minor of a right mind to know what they are doing? Entrapment? Was there more than one victim? Should a bar serve alcohol to a minor? Was this about morality? Was the town to blame? The police force? The parents? He started his car and put the gear into drive.

⌐—···—⌐

ALTHOUGH THE EFFECTS OF the murder would unfold in the weeks that followed, when the lights shut off at the Denville Community Church late that night on September 6, 1953, in many ways, they also went out on the crime itself. It was hidden in the dark corner of the small town's conscience for nearly seventy years. It remains there to this day, still not to be spoken about in public.

The following is James S. Whiton's editorial from the *Denville Herald* from the week after the event, September 3, 1953:

What Caused This Effect?
Modern civilization is anxious to do more for its children than was ever done before in the history of the world. And sometimes it seems to be falling miserably short of the mark.

The *Denville Herald* (eventually the *Citizen*) building (*white building in the center*) on Diamond Spring Road, where John Whiton wrote his editorials. *Denville Historical Society.*

This issue you are reading presents many of the confused and confusing facets of the problem. On one hand it reports that gamma globulin is reserved principally for the protection of the younger victims of polio; that three Explorer Scouts have just come back from a trip to New Mexico; that school systems costing millions of dollars just in this small section of Morris County are about to reopen while a bewildering variety of summer recreation programs come to an end; that a group of adults in Rock Ridge have invested both cash and labor to build a shelter for children at a school bus stop. And on the other, that 13 young men and boys are charged with a brutal, unprovoked murder.

We know that human behavior follows predictable patterns. What facts stand out in the tragedy of youth gone wrong from which we may try to chart a new course?

First, there was a lack of parental control. How else can you explain the fact that a fair-sized group of teenagers were roaming the roads between 11 p.m. and 1 a.m.?

Second, there was idleness, its cumulatively vicious effect at peak after long weeks in which many of the gang were virtually prohibited from any honest employment. Our child labor laws, designed to protect children from sweatshops that were made obsolete by the need for industrial efficiency, have all too often succeeded in denying most teenagers the experience of receiving an honest day's pay for an honest day's work.

A possible third factor, closely allied to both the first and second, is the lack of suitable summer recreation. Note that nearly all the young defendants live in areas not served by any of the lake community clubs with their programs of social and athletic activities. Years ago we tried to interest a service club in developing a swimming pond where children without lake privileges could enjoy similar recreational opportunities. The idea was taken up, and then dropped when the head of a neighboring lake club complained that a free public swimming place would cause his group to lose dues-paying members! The pond is still there—perhaps the idea would get a better reception today. Or does "Suffer little children…" still carry less weight than the need to maintain facilities "for members only"?

We do not ask nor expect that you agree with all the foregoing. It will have accomplished its purpose if it makes you think.[67]

The town was left bewildered and full of questions. How could this happen—and in Denville, of all possible places? It was a happy place where people came to be with families, to relax, have fun and decompress from their busy lifestyles. It was a place where, for a lack of a better phrase, everyone knew your name. When James S. Whiton, the editor of the *Denville Herald*, sat down in front of his typewriter at the newspaper's office at 28 Dimond Spring Road, he was torn. People would want answers. There was so much *good* in the community to report on this week—so many kind actions, specifically by teens, little league players and boy scouts that should have taken precedence. Yet there was the inevitable and unavoidable topic that needed to be mentioned. Was it the parents who allowed their kids to stay out late? Was it the government for not granting enough job opportunities for youths? Or was it the supposedly "greedy" lake communities that only allowed their own private members access to the many activities and amenities they had to offer, leaving all other youths idle in the long summer months? Maybe it was all of the above. One thing was obvious: people needed answers about the causes of juvenile delinquency if the town was to do something about it.

Whiton's editorial was never going to be left unopposed. John M. Franz, an NYU graduate and New York resident who vacationed in Denville with his family every summer from 1942 until eventually moving to town in the early 1980s, was quick with his rebuttal.[68] Two things become very clear from his Mail Bag letter to the editor dated a week after the initial editorial.

One: the people of Denville shared the "grief of these parents," and nobody was going to blame the youths, as "whether the boys are guilty of the crime with which they are charged is for a jury to decide." Two: there existed a perceived feeling of entitlement and pretentiousness, as well as a feeling of us versus them between those who belonged and did not belong to the various lake communities. He said:

> *You suggest that "Suffer little children" carries less weight than the need to maintain the people who took their first chance and organized and invested their savings to combat the conditions which you deplore are partly responsible for these boys and their families needing a second chance. In fact, these organized people are paying a "premium" in club dues and considerable individual effort to make a better community—yet you suggest that they are possibly, one of the "factors" contributing to juvenile delinquency. That sounds like the thief who blamed all his troubles on the fact that his neighbor was honest!*[69]

The summer resident went after the idea that teenagers needed to have summer jobs. According to him, "Why should a fourteen-year-old boy be expected to fill his need for constant activity by being employed for pay? How about 'employing' his energy in recreational activities which are just as plain as fun?"[70]

The answer from the 28 Diamond Spring Road office was swift and to the point. Appearing in the same issue, the editor reiterated his beliefs and highlighted what he thought needed to be addressed in Denville, namely more resources for the town's less privileged, more local businesses willing to hire the young and a bigger sense of town unity though various programs. His rebuttal read:

> *Note 1: Our reference to the short-lived project to establish a free public swimming and waddling beach evidently has been misunderstood by Mr. Franz, we have only admiration and best wishes for those who are willing to invest their savings and devote personal effort to create better facilities for themselves and their fellow club members. Nor have we any quarrel with their insistence that these facilities be reserved for members only. Our criticism was aimed at the dog-in-the-manager attitude of the club official who was not satisfied to maintain his club facilities but who actively opposed, the creation of other, outside facilities which could have been used by less privileged folks who do not have access to the lakes.*

Note 2: We still feel that the child labor laws do deny the chance for honest employment to most teen-agers during the summer. Obviously there aren't enough golf courses to hire all the teenage boys all summer long, even if they all wanted to be caddies, nor are there enough agricultural and "odd jobs" open in this area to occupy all the boys. We have talked with many employers who have had to turn away boys who were anxious to work full time, simply because they were under the age of 18. Does it make sense to "protect" a teenager from the ordinary risks of honest work, only by condemning him to the far greater risks of idleness? Neither have we any quarrel with "recreational activities which are just plain fun," But what boy with any initiative or imagination (and juvenile delinquents often have these qualities in abundance) will be satisfied with spending a whole summer just "having fun?" Does that offer any challenge? It is our honest conviction that the great majority of teen-agers, like the great majority of people generally, find their greatest satisfaction in doing something they feel is genuinely worthwhile, not in simply killing time.

Note 3: The idea of having a full-time paid summer recreation director is appealing, and perhaps it could be worked out. But somewhere along the line it must face the peculiar situation existing in Denville Township. Namely, that we have several lake communities, each of which is a more or less separate unit. Each lake is trying to provide its own program for its young people, with the result that there is less interest in providing a program for the young people who live outside the lake boundaries. This problem might be solved if the governing boards of the several lakes would be willing to work cooperatively with each other and with the people from the center of town and Union Hill. But the solution won't be easy while "For Members Only" stands as a barrier to all the children who don't have lake privileges.
—Ed[71]

While these editorials started the conversation, they did not necessarily provide any solutions. They also exposed some deeper divisions in the seemingly united and quaint community. Others seeking these answers and solutions decided to turn to the town's teenagers themselves. A longtime resident of Cedar Lake, John Zieger, took out an ad in the local paper to offer "a $10 prize for an essay by a teenager on what parents should do to prevent delinquency."[72] It was advertised a week later as "a chance for young people to sound off on what their parents and the community generally can do to help teenagers have fun without getting in trouble."[73]

The new Morris Hills Regional High School in 1953, where the Denville teens attended before another school was built a decade later. *Denville Historical Society.*

While the winner was Marilyn Hopler, a senior at Morris Hills Regional High School—which had just opened its doors for the first time that year— not much is known about the contents of her essay.

5

FINDING FAULT

As the town of Denville created a schedule for the open town hall meetings and forums that were held at the Denville Community Church on Diamond Spring Road, the organizers knew the need for change, but they most certainly could not all agree on what exactly needed to be changed and how. The first of the four, described earlier, was probably the most attended and took place on Sunday, September 6, 1953. It was decided that the fifty-plus people who showed up—parents, teachers and interested citizens—came away "with a better understanding of how complex the problem [was], even if they had no better idea of how to cure it."[74] In the end, the numerous town halls that were led by police officers, psychologists, social agency representatives, students, teachers, business owners, local politicians and local ministry came up with a few reasons that assigned blame to the parents and the individuals as much as the community itself.

"Youth Needs Better Parents, Not Curfew," "Delinquency Panel Feels Parents' Lack of Interest and Official Leniency Are to Blame" and "Curfew Is Not Recommended" screamed off the top of the front pages. The first panel could be described as a success not by the answers that it provided—as there were not many—but by the questions it raised. The initial meeting, which filled the room with concerned citizens, set the precedent for the serious tone, specialization of those involved with the panel and what was to be expected from all future meetings. This was seen through those selection of those running the first event.[75]

One of the *Denville Herald* headlines reporting on the delinquency panel hearings at the Denville Community Church. *From* the Denville Herald, *September 10, 1953.*

Although the neighboring town of Dover had a curfew for its youth, it was decided that such a measure would not work in Denville, as the police department just did not have enough manpower to enforce it. Behind the issue was an even bigger one that took center stage, albeit indirectly. This was the growth of suburbs and the local government's inability to keep up with the change sweeping the nation. When pressed about why areas such as lover's lane, where the murder took place, were not better patrolled, Jenkins highlighted the plight of many small suburban towns of the time—simply not enough police officers. Denville's population had boomed, which was consistent with the growth of suburbia in the post–World War II period. Across the state, "farms became villages almost overnight; villages became towns, towns became cities; fields and orchards in Morris county yielded to new streets and row-on-row of look-alike new houses."[76] With this came overpopulation, inattentiveness and distraction by consumerism, as well as boredom and idleness. The Denville murder became as much about the actual case as it did about the dark side of suburbia. And the town halls were more about how to fight this new national reality.

With the economy booming, many Americans in the early 1950s turned their attention to their jobs and families. Through achieving job security, masses could move to the suburbs, which in turn, symbolized the achievement of the so-called American dream. Denville, New Jersey, like many small suburban towns, offered affordable single-family housing, a growing school system—with a new elementary school and regional high school near completion—a friendly and healthy (lake community) environment for children, and many like-minded neighbors. Concurrently, Americans of the decade also found themselves with loads of leisure time. Most employees worked their forty-hour workweeks and were granted numerous vacation days. More importantly, each household was equipped with many new time-saving devices, such as washing machines and driers, gas-powered lawn mowers and dishwashers. In 1953, the year of the murder, *Forbes Magazine* reported that Americans spent more than $30 billion on leisure goods and activities in the twelve months leading to the study's publication.[77] New consumerism and mass media were right there to provide a new meaning of success—one based on material goods.

As people had more leisure time and more money to spend, they invested in recreational items. In many instances, the things they purchased either led to more leisure time, as was the case with high fidelity record players, barbecue grills and lawn mowers, or to even more distraction, as was the case with the invention and popularity of televisions. The advertising industry capitalized on this newfound consumer freedom and flooded local newspapers, magazines and televisions with ads promoting everything from cigarettes and cereal to cars and even homes. Not everyone, however, had the money or the means to enjoy this new freedom—certainly not on equal terms. It was noted at one of the town forums after the Denville murder that the kids charged with the crime did not live or enjoy the many benefits of being part of any of the town's lake communities. It was further pointed out that this lack of membership created the assumption that they did not possess as much money as those kids whose parents belonged to Denville's private communities. This lack of funds to live in the areas where activities were offered led some citizens to point out the plight of those young men and women of Denville who were left with too much leisure time not by choice but because their own society or even their own town had failed them.

According to the panel of the fourth town hall forum, which this time was led by Denville's twelfth graders from the new Morris Hills High School, living in the suburbs was just downright "boring." It was also pointed out that if one was not into sports or did not belong to any lake community, there truly was nothing to do in the small town. Coupled with parental inattentiveness, the kids felt the drudge of living in the suburbs leading them to wander around town aimlessly. According to the *Denville Herald* from Thursday, October 8, 1953, Denville was almost totally lacking in the kinds of recreational facilities that high school students really wanted, especially judging by their own comments on the issue. "There should be more places for young people to congregate and parents should be more curious about where their children are," stated a Morris Hills senior.[78] She also added that while many people point to the local beaches as a means of recreation, they are tightly closed and "monitored against outsiders."[79] Furthermore, even though there were church halls available in town, there was no necessary parental supervision to actually use them. In short, adults were not willing to volunteer their time.

When asked what was considered recreation, it was stated that "the young people consider recreation [as] something to break the routine of school and homework." It was suggested by another local boy that the Community Church hall invest money in "ping pong tables, shuffleboards, coke machines, and an ice cream stand and a good record player."[80]

One girl was even quoted as saying, "There is nothing here!" She later added that "dancing is popular, but there is no place in town for it. When asked if recreation would help the small percentage of youngsters who get into most trouble, "Miss Hopler [a local high school student] said it would, as they would tend to go where the crowd was."[81] After some elder members in the crowd pushed back against the building of a recreation center, the young panel shot back with, "Crime costs more than a building."[82]

While it might be difficult to see these comments as something other than immature youngsters wanting even more out of their community without being willing to put in the work, it does at least make one curious that it was the one thing the teens chose to point to when asked about what might have brought about the terrible events in their small town barely a month before. Their views correlate with studies of many social critics who diagnosed life in suburbia as monotone, conforming and dreary. Bolstered by Cold War politics of the time, the nuclear family, female domesticity, prized children, perfectly kept lawns and white picket fences became the embodiment of Americanism.

According to historian James A. Henretta of the University of Maryland, "Americans who deviated from prevailing gender and familial norms [of White suburbia] were not only viewed with scorn but were also sometimes thought to be subversive and politically dangerous."[83] These attitudes in turn translated to bland and conforming suburban towns where individualism was spurned and anything out of routine was suspect. This is not an ideal place for lively teenagers trying to find themselves as individuals and ultimately contributing members of American society.

⌐—···—⌐

ONE OF THE MOST striking cultural phenomena to come out of the 1950s was the emergence of a distinct teen culture. With parents too busy conforming to societal expectations and chasing the American dream through consumer spending, their kids found themselves feeling neglected. Being part of the famous baby boomer generation, the teenagers of the 1950s made up the largest single generation in American history. This did not escape corporate market researchers, who identified a separate teen market that was just waiting to be exploited. "Newsweek noted with awe in 1951 that the aggregate of the weekly spending of teenagers was enough to buy 190 million candy bars, 130 million soft drinks, and 230 million sticks of gum." As such, the advertising machine went full force to not only capture their spending money but also their ability to influence family purchases.[84] In the national priority to create secure, safe and orderly communities, teenagers, with their different values, felt marginalized by their parents. "Then the teens started to hear music about their world—songs about high school sweethearts, wild parties and fast cars, sung by other teens. They were hungry for some recognition of their generation, some validation, and when it came [through music, movies and advertising], they embraced it."[85] As showcased through the main character in the Warner Brothers hit *Rebel Without a Cause*, kids blamed their state of confusion and anger on parents' lack of understanding and care.

Denville's eighth grade prom in May 1954. Most of the accused attended the school, some even at the time of the murder, as it served kids up to ninth grade. *Denville Historical Society.*

During the numerous town hall discussions that attempted to assign blame for the Denville murder and the apparent juvenile delinquency that caused it, the topics of parents, parenting and teen neglect were always front and center. During the second forum, on September 13, 1953, Lyle Backer, a member of the town's board of education, was noted for speaking his mind without bothering to protect anyone's feelings. "Better than 50% of parents [in this town] do not give a hoot about their children," he said, adding, "50% of the kids keep out of trouble only by the grace of God."[86] Becker then recalled how "a group of young people tried to get a club started but only one or two parents came out to a meeting attended by 70 of the young people." Similarly, he then told of how he must always give his daughter's friends rides home from parties, though the children's parents could just as easily have driven their own cars and simply chose not to.[87]

William E. Davenport, the superintendent of Denville schools, admitted that the teen complaints about lack of parental care are not necessarily false. And as to whether that would cause children to waver in their morality and commit a crime as heinous as the one that was committed in Denville, he repeated that home influence was the key to all other problems. He added that, for a child, "knowing that he is unwanted is the surest way to fill [him] with hate toward everything."[88]

A week before this, during the first forum, Ms. Helen Moorhead, president of the Denville PTA and a teacher with many years of experience in the locals schools, "roused great interest when she reported the results of a survey made among the town's sixth and eighth graders…where children almost unanimously asked why their parents take no interest in them or what they do, why parents won't even walk half way to bring them home from a dance party at the school."[89]

Chief Jenkins agreed with the statements, saying, "Many delinquents feel unloved and unwanted at home, so they deliberately do wrong things to get some attention." He added, "The source of the trouble is at home.… The day will come when the laws will permit delinquent parents to be fined or jailed."[90]

Home as the key factor was brought up again at the third Denville community forum on September 20, 1953. When asked about the role of church and religion in helping the youth of Denville feel empowered, Reverend Julius Brasher said, "It takes an incredible amount of effort to get volunteers to work with young people," recalling a time when "parents of twenty young people were invited to a meeting…[and] none came."[91]

In one of the later forums, it was mentioned that school doors were locked too much of the time after school hours. When pressed on the issue, a school representative agreed but then stated that "parents should come out to furnish the necessary supervision.…Yet experience has shown that this does not work," as they never volunteer.[92] In fact, the absence of parents in the kids' extracurricular activities led teens to turn elsewhere for role models, namely, television, comic books and rock-and-roll in the later part of the decade. Those other mediums also received the brunt of the blame for kids' lack of morality. The one medium that became the topic of Senate hearings in 1954, mere months after the Denville murder, was comic books.

The nationally televised U.S. Senate hearings, led by Tennessee Democrat Estes Kefauver, brought up concerns of excessive crime, violence and sex in comic books, desensitizing the youth to those issues and in turn encouraging juvenile delinquency.[93] The man who pioneered the crusade against comic books, which he saw as responsible for society's ills, was psychiatrist and author Frederic Wertham. According to an investigative report by Vox, when working in a Harlem hospital that was treating juvenile delinquents, the future author and specialist on the topic noticed many kids and teens reading comic books.[94] Wertham then made it his life's work to prove his belief and findings that young people who read comic books were sexually aggressive, which in turn, led them to commit crimes. Speaking at symposiums and publishing his essays and books, the psychiatrist claimed that "Wonder Woman was a lesbian, Batman and Robin were gay, and comic books were leading children into danger."[95] His views propelled the question of comic books to the public psyche, when, following Kefauver's Senate hearings, Wertham was quoted on the front page of the *New York Times*, saying he was more scared of comic books than he was of Hitler. "Well, I hate to say that, Senator, but I think Hitler was a beginner compared to the comic-book industry…[which] get the children much younger [and]…teach them hatred at the age of 4 before they can read."[96]

The Senate's final report, written by Senator Kefauver, pointed out the "scantily clad women" and the "penchant for violent death" common in comic books aimed at teenagers.[97] These findings might have been the reason for the comic book industry self-censoring through the creation of the Comics Code. But the politicians were up against a much larger behemoth in the power of television. Many critics of the new mass medium complained that the youth of America could now visually see violence happening on television, something that was just not accessible before. This was not necessarily an incorrect assumption, as in 1947, there were 7,000 television sets in American homes, and by 1950, that number grew to 7.3 million.[98] Per Nielsen Media Research, *Dragnet* was one of the top shows on air in 1953 and was revered for its real portrayal of violence, delinquency and crime.[99] It was also, presumably, based on real events, and each episode was a reenactment of a real police case. This was also the year that the Western *Gunsmoke* burst into the television scene and quickly became a teenage boys' favorite. One of the factors that made it so was its portrayal of violence, which, through its gunfights and bar brawls, seemed to mirror the darker side of human nature. There is no arguing with the fact that between television and comic books, kids and young adults had much better access to what some might call the glorification and popularization of violence. But assigning blame to a TV show or a comic book for turning teenagers in a small town toward murder does seem a bit far-fetched.

ONE OF THE MOTIVES provided by the Morris County Prosecutor's Office of Ross E.M. was the fact that he was homosexual.[100] The year of the murder, a number of controversial studies released by Indiana University zoologist Alfred Kinsey revealed the struggle between older moral traditions and newly found freedoms of suburban Americans. Taking a scientific approach to his study and placing morality aside, his books, *Sexual Behavior in the Human Male* and *Sexual Behavior in the Human Female*, became national bestsellers, with the latter selling 270,000 copies in the first month of its publication in 1953.[101] In his books was one of his most controversial findings—that homosexuality was a lot more common in the United States than the public suspected. "Although the American Psychiatric Association...officially [defined] homosexuality as a mental illness in 1952, Kinsey's research found that 37 percent of men had engaged in some form of homosexual activity by early adulthood, as had 13 percent of women," with a further claim that "10 percent of American men were exclusively homosexual."[102] This was a major change in conversation, as the topic of homosexuality, was up to that point, avoided at all costs, especially in the media.

When the silence was broken by Kinsey's studies, "all major religions considered [homosexuality] sinful and immoral, psychiatrists considered it a serious mental disorder that needed to be treated, and nearly every state had laws criminalizing it, many calling for prison terms for 'convicted' homosexuals."[103] The two largest weekly news magazines of the 1950s,

Time and *Newsweek*, together published a total of just twenty-one articles about homosexuality, with almost universal criticisms of it, including words such as "abominable, degenerate, disgusting, evil, extreme medical disorder, immoral, sex criminal, and wicked."[104] When looking at the stark statistics, it becomes evident that homosexuality was still vilified, and if the press was indeed a reflection of public beliefs, it puts a different spin on crimes of the time in which the victim was homosexual.

In his book *Indecent Advances: A Hidden History of True Crime and Prejudice Before Stonewall*, released in 2019, James Polchin, a cultural historian and professor of global liberal studies at New York University, analyzed newspapers from 1920 to 1960 in search of crimes against gay or presumed gay men.[105] In light of his work, the Denville murder is very consistent with other crimes during its time, yet it is also so different from them. According to Polchin, in the mid-twentieth century, gay and bisexual men were especially vulnerable to violence, but crimes against them were rarely reported as such in the press. As was the case with the Denville murder, where newspaper headlines ranged from "Man Found Slain in Lover's Lane" to "13 Held in Denville Murder Case" and "Hold 2 for Murder; Robbery One Motive," crimes were rarely reported as ones against gay men. As such, "Polchin searched newspaper archives for terms like 'man found murdered in hotel' or 'sailor found murdered in park,' and sifted through the resulting articles for what [he called] 'undercurrents of queer experience'—details about where or how the victim and killer met, for example."[106] Another thing that the author found interesting through his research was the fact that in many of the stories the victims were married and had kids. This was also the case with the Denville murder, as Ross E.M. was reported to have been engaged to a woman at the time of his murder.

There was one specific story of a man in 1930s who moved to the New York area from Virginia. When he tried to pick up two men he met at a bar, they lured him out and brutally beat him to death.[107] The story goes on to point out that, similar to the Denville case, when the men responsible were arrested and went to court, the victim's family didn't pursue the case in the media because they were fearful of "the publicity that would come with it, making known their son's homosexuality."[108] As such, the men responsible for committing the crime met with lesser charges. The similarity of the Denville murder to the overall pattern of crimes against homosexual people in the 1950s is uncanny—even down to the family reaction. In Ross E.M.'s case, the family was very well known in their home state of North Carolina, and there is no mention of the murder in their local town's newspapers.

But there is indeed one component of the crime that perhaps challenges its classification as a sex or hate crime—the issue of a grown man attempting to illicit sexual favors from a minor.

While we have made major advancements in bringing awareness to sexual abuse of children and its damaging physical and psychological consequences, the United States of the 1950s was much different. In fact, it is extraordinary how recently the sexual abuse of children began to be taken seriously. "Not until 1974, when Congress passed the Child Abuse Prevention and Treatment Act, were states required to establish reporting requirements in suspected cases."[109] A longtime Canadian expert on the issue, psychologist William L. Marshall, stated that by 1960, "there was so little professional literature available on people who sexually abused minors that 'you could read it all in one morning.'"[110] The 1950s was a time when discussing emotions was seen as coddling—something that was directly referenced in the Denville town halls. As such, the boys in the Denville 13 case might have been reluctant to go to their parents about the issue of a man making advances toward them.

The discussion at the third session of the Denville Community Church on Sunday, September 20, 1953, centered on how social and welfare agencies could help parents and children. It was led by professionals in their fields, Dr. T.A. Newlin, the president of the Morris County Mental Health Association; Ms. Jane Moore of the Morris County Welfare Board and Children's Protective Service; Ms. Eleanor Levy, Denville welfare director; and Franklin Parks, executive secretary of the Family Service of Morris County.[111] Apart from the particulars of the discussion, it became evident that the climate in which the Denville boys lived was not conducive to sharing their feelings. There was also no place outside of the home where the kids could turn to if they wanted to talk about their feelings. The Morris County Mental Health Association, noted for being one of the first health associations of its kind in the state and even the nation, was just getting organized. Dr. Newlin spoke of the difficulty of his organization in getting started and the cases of abuse, abandonment and neglect, and the mental effects that came out of them still "having such a hush hush attitude."[112] His goal for the agency was to "act as the [Morris] county exchange to bring together persons who [needed] help."[113] He lamented how many people did not come forward when it came to discussing their feelings. A local resident who spoke at the question-and-answer session after the panel said, "Police officers generally seem to have a low opinion of the way the professional social workers 'coddle' the young… and asked what police should do when they find a young teenager roaming the streets after midnight."[114] No answer was given, but none was really needed. The question spoke volumes on the attitude toward "coddled" teens who couldn't handle adversity.

In the end, the four town halls did not accomplish much on figuring out what might have caused such a serious crime to be committed in such a small town and by such young individuals. It did, however, bring to light some important points that might make one understand the climate in which such an event might have been possible in the first place—not only in Denville, New Jersey, but also in any suburban town across the state and the nation. Reflecting on the forums, the *Denville Herald* editor wrote, "Out of thousands of words spoken by dozens of persons in the course of the forums on juvenile problems held at the Denville Community Church, it is gradually becoming clear that Denville has made a good start...but is sadly lacking in many respects."[115]

Based on closer analysis, it becomes evident that while the blame for the event cannot be assigned to one specific factor, there are many that likely contributed to it. There was the fear of homosexuality, which at the time was officially condemned. Similarly, there was an unspoken rule for young boys to hide their emotions and fears by dealing with their issues instead of complaining about them. This coupled with the monotony of the newly established suburban towns, parental negligence, consumer culture and fiscal inability for all to participate in the so-called American dream, and the scene, if not set for such a criminal act, was at least properly cast and staged.

6
REQUIEM

For those involved in the crime, life moved on. They got married, had children, grandchildren and even great-grandchildren. At the time of this writing, all but one have passed away, and three are unaccounted for. It is very difficult to assign blame for the crime, as there are so many layers when it comes to this murder. There is the obvious baiting of the victim, but there are also the immoral and illegal actions of the victim himself, attempting to seduce minors, providing them with alcohol for consumption and allowing them to drive under the influence and underage. Then there is the question of motive. Homosexuality at the time was vilified, and crimes associated with it were swept under the rug and forgotten. Of course, there is also the age of the accused and the psychological implications of minors still not being mature enough to make the right decisions, as well as being easily peer-pressured and persuaded. This might have been the case here, with the oldest member of the gang being the only one sent to jail.

Murder is never something that should be taken lightly, and in this case, it seems that there were many casualties and not just Ross E.M. There were the kids who did something terrible that would haunt them for the rest of their lives. There were also the families of all of those involved. The parents of the victim, having to grieve the loss of their son, and the parents of the boys and young men involved. They had to face the scorn of the entire town and even the nation, while at the same time remaining supportive of their kids in light of the terrible events they had played a part in. Only those involved would know the pain and weight of having to carry with them the

One of the crates containing the original *Denville Herald* newspapers from the 1950s, located at the Denville Historical Society. The entire decade is missing just one issue—the one that detailed the murder in lover's lane. *Photo by author.*

memories of that fateful night. On the other hand, we can at least take a glimpse into their lives after the event. What can be seen is that most of the Denville 13 lived on to become productive members of society—at least those who were able to be located at the time of this research.

Richard M. eventually enlisted in the U.S. Marine Corps, where he became private first class from Camp Pendleton. He passed away in a tragic private plane accident in California only five years after the Denville murder in April 1958. Jerre H. eventually moved to Charleston, South Carolina, where he joined the U.S. Navy and served in the Korean War. After he returned, he worked as a railroad signalman. He married and started a family in 1959. He passed away in 2011. Philip K. moved to Idaho and then Arizona. Not much is known about his life, apart from the fact that he died of natural causes in 2000. The same goes for his younger brother, John K., who in his adulthood relocated to Long Island, New York, where he died in 2009. Russell C., one of the youngest members of the group, made quite a name for himself in the motorcycle racing circuit and is honored in the Motorcycle Museum Hall of Fame. He eventually became a car mechanic. He passed away from cancer while living in California in 2014. Burl C., another fourteen-year-old of the group, got married and moved a few towns away. He was a custodian at a local university in New Jersey, for twenty-five years. He passed away in 2015.

Edwin R., who worked for Howmet Corporation in Dover and was very involved in the U.S. Mineral Wool Union, was dedicated to helping the local youth. He was known as a beloved coach of multiple youth sports, including baseball, football and wrestling. Mr. R. was also commended for a lifetime work of sponsoring, supporting and organizing many youth organizations and athletics in his community. He passed away in Florida in 2015. Donald F., who, according to his obituary from 2007, had at some point changed his name, got married and lived locally for the remainder of his life. He passed away in St. Claire's Hospital in Denville. Not much is known about William W., apart from the fact that he also got married and started a family after moving to Santa Clara, California. He died in Sacramento, California, in 2017.

Research on Richard K., Edwin D. and most importantly George C.—the only one committed to prison for the murder—leads to a dead end. Apart from articles on the murder, there are no further records pertaining to the three men. It is possible that they changed their names in their adult lives.

The only member of the group who is still alive at the time of this writing is Lars O. It is partially in respect to him that this work omits all last names. A Google search brings up an interesting case. In 1956, Mr. O. sued the Denville Police and the Department of Law and Public Safety for the return of his fingerprints. In the lawsuit, Lars O. contended that it was improper for his fingerprints to be taken during his arrest and was seeking the court to require the fingerprints to be turned over so they could be destroyed. It was further pointed out by the court that the statue, R.S. 53:1–15, provided for fingerprints to be taken at the arrest of a person charged with an indictable offense, but since Lars was underage, he could not be charged with an indictable offense. So, there was no right, much less duty, to take his fingerprints.[116] Rightfully so, he won the case.

The two Denville police officers who were directly involved with the investigation, Chief Harry B. Jenkins and Captain Arthur Strathman, never again publicly spoke about the event. Years later, in 1967, when he was getting ready to retire, Strathman provided an interview for the *Morris County Record*, reminiscing on his time as a police officer. When asked about his time on the force and the most trying period during his thirty-year career, the captain and chief (taking over for Harry B. Jenkins) exclaimed, "A policeman's lot was not an unhappy one in those days....We got more or less the same type of calls, but not so many....Besides in [Denville]...people went to bed with the chickens and stayed out of trouble."[117] The article went on to say that "Strathman's recollections of his 30 year tour of duty are so unruffled that he's hard put to remember specific incidents."[118] This is very interesting considering that Arthur was the first police officer at the scene of one of the most controversial murders in his state's history. But then again, he was most definitely sticking with the script that defined the Denville 13 murder case for years to come—it never happened.

CHIEF JENKINS FOUND HIMSELF tired again. He was once more facing a crowd, this time at the town hall. The year was 1962. He had, just a few days before, shockingly handed in his resignation to the township committee he was now facing. He sat there listening to the numerous statements by concerned citizens who did not want him to be allowed to leave. His mind might have brought him back to a different time where he sat in front of the town's citizens. The town was so different now. There were numerous sports fields and parks, athletic clubs, plans for a vocational school in the process of being approved and not a single murder or serious crime committed since that fateful day in 1953. He looked up, as if waking up from a daze, in time to hear a commissioner read his resignation statement:

> *I submit this resignation with the firm conviction that I have performed my duties as Chief of Police of the Township of Denville in a sincere, conscientious and thorough manner and to the full extent that the rules and regulations promulgated by the Township Committee governing the Police Department permit me to function. Inasmuch as the rules and regulations place the matter of discipline of the Police Dept. in the hands of the Police Committee and not in the Chief of Police, I have decided that I cannot serve with the honor and respect due that office I prefer not to serve at all.*[119]

After reading the document and acknowledging the acceptance of petitions bearing some five hundred signatures supporting the police chief and hearing out numerous town citizens, the committee closed the meeting by accepting the disgruntled and tired chief's resignation.

But the town did not forget Jenkins, the cool and collected police officer who assured them almost a decade before that everything would be all right. "Apparently stunned by the verdict, most of the 75 onlookers, who jammed the hall, expressed their dissatisfaction verbally. As the meeting adjourned, many lined up to shake hands with Jenkins and to offer their opinions of action taken. Others marched to the bench and heaped abuse on Committee members."[120]

After leaving the hall that night, Harry B. Jenkins got in his own private car. Once more, he took a deep breath. It all seemed so familiar. But this time he knew that he did all right. Maybe not this day in 1962, but he knew that he did all right by his people on a different day, one that now seemed so long ago.

One of the most talked-about issues in the town after the events of August 31, 1953, was the lack of supervision of young adults and the inability of the town to provide them with any meaningful activities and clubs to occupy their time. The same went for their inability to curb the negative effects of idleness. Today's Denville could never be accused of the same things. Constantly ranking at the top of the charts of best family-friendly towns to live in by the *New Jersey Monthly Magazine*, Denville is bursting with family-oriented activities, parks, clubs and youth sports. One of the determining factors looked at by researchers at Leflein Associates, which conducts research in the towns, is "lifestyle factor," in which Denville continuously excels.[121] If not for anything else, the changes that Denville made with relation to the issues that came up after the crime show how the small town took it on itself to strive to be a model suburban town—one that could one day be called the state's Best Place to Live.[122]

Following the Denville murder, an ad appeared in *Denville Herald*, inviting boys to "Organize a New Sport Club."[123] Perhaps not so coincidentally, the ad called for boys ages fourteen and older to come to a meeting. The meeting was to take place at the house of William Gardner, the chairman of the township recreational committee and the namesake for the eventual sports complex Gardner's Field, near the center of town. The idea was to form a boys' social, athletic and recreational group with the Knights of Columbus. The meeting was very successful, with twenty-seven kids reporting. In a few weeks, the official meeting place was chosen to be the local Knights of Columbus hall, and even the town's mayor attended the first meeting.[124] An article in the local paper provided some insight into the newly dubbed Denville Youth Organization's events. They included scrimmage sessions at the local Imperial Field and dances at the hall.[125] It is apparent that the citizens of the small town took to implementing changes for the kids almost immediately. Although a small gesture in comparison to the events of late

A photo of Denville PAL's first induction ceremony. The creation of the local Police Athletic League was spurred on by the events of the summer of 1953. *Denville Historical Society.*

August, it at least showed that the local government and its people did listen to their kids' concerns, even though the effects of these activities on fixing juvenile crime was not clear.

Concurrent with the new youth organization, the Denville Police Athletic League (PAL) was organized barely a month after the murder. The initial cohort was made of forty boys from town and was advised by police officers John Kelly and Stanley Slavinski.[126] The swearing in was organized to take place in the Denville Theatre in the center of town, with an anticipated membership exceeding three hundred.[127] In the coming month, the citizens of Denville would find themselves opening their doors to young men walking house to house appealing for funds for the new organization.[128] The dues were set at fifty cents per year, and arrangements were made to use the Morris Hills High School's gymnasium for winter activities on Tuesday nights.[129] For a one-dollar donation, willing town patrons would become honorary members. The ceremony took place at 10:00 a.m. on a sunny but quite chilly November morning. The large group of boys assembled and exceeded the initially predicted number of inductees. They were all between the ages of ten and twenty-one.

Mayor John C. Hogan (*center*) with other members of the town council. The mayor was present at all of the hearings and the first two meetings of the delinquency panel meetings. *Denville Historical Society.*

"Keep working for your church, your religious duties and those things which you know are right and you can't go wrong," Judge David A. Nimmo of Hudson County told the Denville boys gathered in the Denville Theatre for the first mass induction ceremony of Denville's newly formed PAL.[130] The local paper pointed out how the PAL and similar organizations working with and for the youth have been responsible for a decrease in juvenile delinquency in other towns. It was hoped that the same would happen for

Denville. During the ceremony, the Mayor Hogan revealed that a girls' division of the PAL would be started as soon as the boys' group was well underway, and he described the plans of leaders to obtain a Quonset hut, which would be the group's headquarters for athletic and social activities.[131]

Another sign of the town and its people responding to the unfortunate events of late summer could be seen in citizen involvement in community affairs. The Denville PTA's membership for the school year 1953–54 jumped to an astonishing nearly 100 percent parent involvement.[132] For all young people to be able to partake in the new athletic activities, local churches got together and held a sport equipment sale and donation night, where all kinds of outgrown equipment, such as ice skates, bicycles, scooters, football uniforms, skis, boots and overshoes, could be acquired at either low or no cost by those less fortunate members of the town.[133] This all-in, it takes a village attitude was also seen though the local reports of higher church attendance by Denville families. The Denville Community Church reported doubling its Sunday mass attendance since the beginning of the month. The membership of the Methodist Youth Fellowship group of young people also doubled in that same time.[134]

ACCORDING TO NICHE.COM, A data analysis website that uses dozens of public data sources including the Department of Education, U.S. census, FBI and the IRS, Denville, as of 2020, ranks as one of the best towns to live in and raise a family in the state of New Jersey.[135] It ranks in the top one hundred list of the Best Suburbs to Raise a Family in New Jersey, as well as Best Suburbs to Live in New Jersey and Suburbs with the Best Public Schools in New Jersey. It is also in the top 10 percent of the Best Places to Raise a Family in America. Calculated annually per 100,000 residents, the national number for assault and murder is 288 and 6, respectively; for Denville, it is 0 in both categories.[136] These statistics are not surprising to anyone who lives, has lived or has ever visited the small town.

An argument could be made that it was the events of the summer of 1953, nearly seventy years ago, that made the town what it is today. Near today's town center is an outdoor complex of soccer fields, football fields, baseball fields, tennis courts and a beautiful playground. This is not a twenty-first-century fad of installing turf fields for commercial youth travel sports. The complex honors the name of Doctor Gardner, who shortly after

Left: William "Doc" Gardner, one of Denville's most active volunteers of all time. He was the founder of Denville Little League and a proponent of youth activities and sports in the town. The sports complex Gardner Field is named after him. *Denville Historical Society.*

Below: The Gardner Field sports complex, dedicated in 1958 and built because of the need for recreation for Denville's children that came out of the town forums, is a mile away from the 1953 murder scene. *Denville Historical Society.*

the murder in the 1950s, tried to organize a town recreational club. For the remainder of his life, the man championed youth sports and even donated his own land to the creation of what became Gardner's Field. This was in the 1970s, not the 2000s. The PAL has flourished to now offer multiple recreational sports and charitable programs, ranging from basketball to softball and even cheerleading. One citizen recently summarized the town as having "an abundance of activities and events…[and] a family-oriented atmosphere."[137] The Rotary Club invites the children to meet Santa every year at no charge, and it happens every evening for a month so that no one feels like they cannot make it to see him, even the kids of working parents. It is nearly impossible to walk downtown and not be greeted with a warm smile or a hello. Police officers greet the children and frequently visit the schools to educate the young public about safety. It truly is a very quaint town. But if modern rankings had existed in 1953, Denville probably would have ranked just as high. So, how could something as bad as a murder ostensibly committed by thirteen teenagers happen in a town such as Denville? The bottom line is that it could have been any town at any time.

Social historian James Gilbert wrote in his extensive study on juvenile delinquency of the 1950s that the very topic was a familiar idea expressed many times in American history prior to and after the decade. "It was old because it rested on a history of controversy practically as ancient as the misbehavior of youth; it was new because the media in the 1950s… represented something almost revolutionary in the history of mass culture and its impact on American Society."[138] So, the debate over the mass culture's effects on children is as old of a worry today as it was in the 1950s, especially with the rise of social media. It would be impossible to point to one factor that led to or resulted in Ross E.M.'s death. Was it vice, youth, poverty, boredom, parents, town or police? The only thing we do know is that some people, probably without being prompted, took it upon themselves to turn the page on the murder. Some of it was deliberate—choosing to not publish anything about it or hide what was published—and some not so much. Denville chose to not speak up. It did not forget, but it learned and moved on.

The feeling at the time was probably best summarized by Leo Hockstein, the owner of Anchor Supply hardware store in Denville. A month after the Denville murder, the proprietor took out a quarter-page ad in the local paper, titled "Is Murder Ever Justified?" In it he wrote, "We should spend far more on prevention of crime than on its punishment, and when punishment is necessary, the emphasis should be [and only when agreed by psychologists that the offender should not be in custody for the rest of his life] on rehabilitation of the criminal....We are the state, and we are responsible for what the state does."

All of the teenagers went on to live their lives—some for longer than others. Only one young adult—the only one who had a history of serious criminal behavior—took the blame for the murder and went to jail for it. In the end, the town of Denville, its people and the local and state judicial system took a gamble on the rest of the boys. And from what could be proven, it was the right call. Thus as the question of murder ever being justified will continue to be debated, perhaps we can all agree that forgiveness just might be.

EPILOGUE

NOVEMBER 9, 1953

Superior Court of New Jersey in Morristown, Before Honorable Donald M. Waesche

The long day was finally coming to a close. But with most of the boys being referred to juvenile court to await their sentencing in ten days' time, in a sense, it was not quite over. It was certainly not over for the parents who had to go back and face the social scrutiny of their small community. For the family of Ross E.M., although none of them attended that day, the absence of their son for all remaining days would remind them that it would never be over. And for the boys themselves, the nightmare of constant guilt was just getting started. Perhaps it was at that moment that someone decided to ease everyone's pain and attempt to erase the event from Denville's conscience through purposeful omission of the event from the town's press and public records. We can only assume.

"Are all the defendants here?" asked Judge Waesche.

"Yes, Your Honor."

"Before the defendants are taken back to jail, I want to speak to them briefly about the law with which they have had this experience—a very unpleasant experience."

"Will the defendants please rise when I speak to them all?" The boys rose and William W. could not hold back his tears, sobbing, he put his face in his hands. "If you are uncomfortable [William] you had better sit down."

Wiping away his tears, the young man answered, "No, I will stand."

The judge proceeded:

> *Well, to you 13 Young Men, all of you were charged with the crime of murder, of which I am sure you are well aware of—a crime which is the worst crime of all crimes. You may not be guilty as you have been charged. You have not been tried for that crime, and you will not be tried. In fact, a plea of guilty to a lower grade of crime has been or probably will be accepted in each case, depending upon each one's own individual action, intent and state of minds at the time of the crime. And by that I mean, depending upon the part that each of you took in the offense which led up to and which caused the death of this decedent.*
>
> *That is the reason why the Prosecutor has examined each of your cases separately and has presented each of your cases separately to the Court, so that in each case you would receive individual consideration according to the offense that you committed.*
>
> *I am sure you all realize that the law which you have confessed violating is many, many years old. It is much older that I am; it is much older than any of us. The Chief of Police, Mr. Jenkins, and the Chief of Police, Mr. Rorich, of Rockaway, they did not make this law. The Prosecutor did not make it. I did not make it. The law applies to you, and to me, and to them, all alike. There is no difference.*
>
> *Whoever violates the law is punished by the law according to his guilt. And by that I mean, you are not punished by the police, or by the Prosecutor, or by the Court. It is our duty, as a matter of law, to enforce the law. It is the law that was violated; it is the law which punished. No one—no one at all—has a special privilege to commit a crime.*
>
> *It is, therefore, no excuse for a defendant to say, "I am a juvenile." If you commit a crime, it makes no difference whether you are an adult or a juvenile; and I think that to plead that you are a juvenile as the only defense that you would have, and seek to hide behind your age, is the act*

only of a coward. You are afraid of what you have done. However, the law intends to treat everybody fairly. When I say "everybody," I mean young people and old people. The law does not seek to impose punishment in excess of that which the offense justly warrants. Nor does the law pamper offenders.

Our Constitution, your Constitution, the Constitution that you have learned about in school, says that cruel and unusual punishments shall not be inflicted upon anyone.

So, if you violate the law, you are punished by the law, and it makes no difference whether you are a juvenile or an adult.

However, again I say to you that the law is made for your benefit, for my benefit, for the benefit of all of us.

The Constitution, our Constitution, says the government is instituted for the protection, for the security and for the benefit of all of us; and, therefore, you have a right to use the law for your benefit and for your protection, use it justly for those purposes.

And the law, of course, is for the benefit of juveniles, as well as for the benefit of older people. And that is the reason why the law has provided for a Juvenile Court, so that young people who find themselves in trouble may have a court of their own in which to be tried. That is fair; that is as it should be.

And it is for that reason that the law has said that a person under the age of 16 years is incapable of committing a crime. The law means by that, that a boy under the age of 16 years cannot have any intent to commit a crime, because of his youth.

Now, it is only fair that the law says that in favor of young people—not only in favor of you boys who are here, but in favor of all young people.

If you are tried for your offense—and again let me say the law does not excuse you from your offense; it only tries to treat that offense fairly, considering all of the circumstances—if you are tried in the Juvenile Court, there is no record of that trial; and if you have made an error, and if you are really sorry for that error, it means that you will never have a record that will haunt you for the rest of your lives.

If an adult commits a crime, he is tried here in open court, and a record of his crime is made available to the public, where it can be examined for the rest of his days by the whole world.

As I said to you, it has seemed that, that is not fair to young people. Because young people have not the years of experience of an adult, and it is not fair to expect as much from a young person as it is from an older person.

But, again let me say that it does not mean you are excused for your offenses; it only means that the law, endeavor to treat fairly.

Now, you have probably heard it said that juvenile delinquency is the fault of the parents. Sometimes that is true, but it is not always true. Some young people have no parents, and sometimes young people will not listen to their parents. But even in cases where parents are to blame for neglecting their children, the law does not excuse the child for any violation thereof merely because of the neglect of his parents. You are still held accountable for your offenses against the law.

It is true that the parent has a very great duty to his child or children. The community also has a very great duty to the young people of the community.

Adults are responsible for the moral training of young people. Young people have no other place to look for guidance. That is necessarily so.

But again, let me remind you that under no circumstances can young people violate the law and escape punishment for their offense against the law, because their parents or their community or somebody else have been negligent in their duties.

Each of you has a future ahead of you. In one or two cases, you are 14 years of age, 15, 16, years of age. You, of course, do not realize it now, what the years ahead of you hold, but you know that if you live an average life, you are going to live to 60 years of age—perhaps 4 times the number of years that you have already lived. It is a long ways ahead. You have it within your power to make those years ahead of you good or make them bad. It is primarily, almost entirely, up to you.

Of course, you expect, I am sure, to be punished for your offense. I want you to realize that you brought this on yourselves. I hope that you also realize that, with proper effort on your part, you can work out of this. I hope you also realize that if you do not work out of this, if you continue to violate the law, that the years ahead of you will be very, very hard and difficult. That is just as sure as is the sky above you.

This offense with which you all have been charged, to which you have pleaded guilty, this happening has not only shocked your community, it has shocked your County and the State.

It is very hard, very difficult, to look in your faces and realize that you have had any part in this shocking offense. You look to be like normal American boys. I believe that you can be. I think that it is a hardship on those who have been forced to bring you to justice. It is not a thing that any of us like to do.

I am sure that, if you make your fair effort to overcome what has happened, insofar as you can, that your parents ought to under any circumstances give you all the help they can, and that your community do what it can. I think, if you try hard, with everything that you can give on your part, I think then you have a right to expect such help.

I did not want to let you leave Court today without having something to say to you about this.

You will again come before me [in ten days]. That may be the last time you will ever see me, or I will ever see you, or that I will ever have a chance to say anything to you. I think that I should take this opportunity to make clear to you, if I can, your position today before the Bar, and to make clear to you that, while things now look to you rather blue and discouraging, you are young, you can overcome it, and that doing so depends upon you.

I do not want any young person of Morris County to feel that, because he is young, he can do just about as he pleases where the law is concerned. He cannot. And I hope that your experience will be a lesson to all of them, that they will all realize what is expected of them as young people.

The Honorable Donald M. Waesche took off his glasses and placed them on the papers in front of him. He rubbed his eyes, shielding his face with his hand. He then looked up, took a deep breath and said, "Have the defendants leave the court room. We will take a short recess."

THE END

NOTES

Introduction

1. "Man Found Slain in Lover's Lane in Denville," *Morristown Daily Record*, August 31, 1953.
2. "13 to Be Arraigned for Murder," *Morristown Daily Record*, October 17, 1953.

Chapter 1

3. "What Happened During World War 2," American Historical Association. https://www.historians.org.
4. Ibid.
5. "Organized Action Being Rallied to Meet Problem of Juvenile Delinquency," *Denville Herald*, July 1, 1943.
6. Ibid.
7. Ibid.
8. Ibid.
9. Ibid.
10. Ibid.
11. Ibid.
12. "Police Nab Two Boys on Theft Charge," *Denville Herald*, January 1, 1952.

13. "Local Youths Face Stolen Car Charges," *Denville Herald*, September 25, 1952.

14. "Local Youths Sentenced," *Denville Herald*, October 2, 1952.

15. "Terry Pharmacy Robbed of $400," *Denville Herald*, January 8, 1953.

16. "Three Youths' Crime Career Ends in Court," *Denville Herald*, March 19, 1953.

17. "7 is to 6,000 As...," *Denville Herald*, April 2, 1953.

18. Ibid.

19. "Bad Apples or Bad Barrels? Zimbardo on the 'Lucifer Effect'" Association for Psychological Science, https://www.psychologicalscience.org.

Chapter 2

20. Mildred Lawrence Gill, *Denville Days* (Denville, NJ: Board of Education Township of Denville, 1955), 73.

21. Charles M. toeLaer, *Reflections of Denville* (Denville, NJ: Redmond Press, 1988), 88.

22. Vito Bianco, *Denville* (Charleston SC: Arcadia Publishing, 2001), 7.

23. *Passaic Herald News*, August 31, 1953.

24. *Hackensack Record*, August 31, 1953.

25. *Morristown Daily Record*, September 3, 1953.

26. Autopsy Records of Ross Midgette. Morris County Prosecutor's Office, PDF (accessed through Open Public Records Act Request, March 17, 2020).

27. Ibid.

28. *Morristown Daily Record*, August 31, 1953.

29. *Gaffney Ledger*, September 5, 1953.

30. *Morristown Daily Record*, August 31, 1953.

31. Ibid.

32. *Gaffney Ledger*, September 5, 1953.

33. U.S. WWII Draft Cards Young Men, 1940–1947, Ancestry.com.

34. *Morristown Daily Record*, August 31, 1953.

35. *Gaffney Ledger*, September 5, 1953.

36. *Morristown Daily Record*, September 3, 1953.

37. "Morris Indicts 13 Youths in Killing," *Passaic Herald News*, October 17, 1953.

38. *Morristown Daily Record*, September 3, 1953.

39. "Rahway Prison Has Lengthy History of Grievances," *New York Times*, November 26, 1971.

40. *Morristown Daily Record*, September 3, 1953.

41. Ibid.

42. Ibid.

43. Ibid.

44. *Passaic Herald News*, September 2, 1953.

45. Ibid.

46. *Philadelphia Inquirer*, August 31, 1953.

47. *Morristown Daily Record*, September 3, 1953.

48. *Passaic Herald News*, September 2, 1953.

49. *Morristown Daily Record*, September 3, 1953.

50. "1934. Appendix D—Grounds for Judicial Deportation," United States Department of Justice Archives, https://www.justice.gov.

51. *Morristown Daily Record*, September 4, 1953.

52. Ibid.

53. Ibid.

54. Ibid.

55. Ibid.

56. Ibid.

57. *Morristown Daily Record*, October 17, 1953.

58. "Slaying Trial Called Off," *New York Times*, November 10, 1953.

59. Ibid.

60. "13 Defendants Change Pleas, Avoid Trials," *Denville Herald*, November 12, 1953.

61. Ibid.

62. "Murder Case Disposed of Last Friday," *Denville Herald*, November 26, 1953.

63. "Youths in Denville Murder Sentenced; One Goes to Prison," *News*, November 21, 1953.

64. Ibid.

Chapter 4

65. U.S. Census, 1950, https://www2.census.gov.

66. Pamphlet for the board of education meeting to propose the creation of Riverview School, October 1950, Denville Historical Society Collection.

67. "What Caused This Event," editorial, *Denville Herald*, September 3, 1953.

68. John M. Franz, "Obituary," *Brattleboro Reformer*, July 2, 1996.

69. "Mail Bag: To the Editor," *Denville Herald*, September 10, 1953.

70. Ibid.

71. Ibid.

72. "Mt. Tabor Notes: Offer Prize for Essay," *Denville Herald*, September 10, 1953.

73. "Unclassified: John Zieger Essay," *Denville Herald*, September 17, 1953.

Chapter 5

74. "Youth Needs Better Parents, Not Curfew," *Denville Herald*, September 10, 1953.

75. Ibid.

76. John T. Cunningham, *New Jersey: A Mirror on America* (Florham Park, NJ: Afton Publishing Company, 1978), 326.

77. Gerald A. Danzer, *The Americans* (Orlando, FL: Holt McDougal, 2012), 851.

78. "Recreation Center Seems What Teenagers Want," *Denville Herald*, October 8, 1953.

79. Ibid.

80. Ibid.

81. Ibid.

82. Ibid.

83. James A. Henretta, *American History* (Boston: Bedford St. Martin, 2016), 752.

84. Ibid., 750.

85. Richard Powers, "The Life of a 1950s Teenager," Social Dance at Stanford, http://socialdance.stanford.edu.

86. "Forum Speakers Question Whether Leniency Is Help," *Denville Herald*, September 17, 1953.

87. Ibid.

88. Ibid.

89. "Youth Needs Better Parents, Not Curfew," *Denville Herald*, September 10, 1953.

90. Ibid.

91. Ibid.

92. "Recreation Center Seems What Teenagers Want," *Denville Herald*, October 8, 1953.

93. Henretta, *American History*, 757.

94. Alex Abad-Santos, "The Insane History of How American Paranoia Ruined and Censored Comic Books," Vox, March 13, 2015, https://www.vox.com.

95. Ibid.

96. Ibid.

97. Henretta, *American History*, 757.

98. Ibid., 749.

99. Cynthia Johnson, *Bowling, Beatniks, and Bell-Bottoms: Pop Culture of 20th and 21st Century America* (Detroit, MI: Gale, 2012), 811.

100. *Morristown Daily Record*, September 3, 1953.

101. Henretta, *American History*, 756.

102. Ibid.

103. "Straight from the Closet," *Thistle*, July 4, 2000, https://www.mit.edu.

104. Ibid.

105. Anna North, "Queer True Crime Stories of the Past Show How the Press Stoked Fear of Gay Man," Vox, June 11, 2019, https://www.vox.com.

106. Ibid.

107. Ibid.

108. Ibid.

109. Steven Mintz, "Placing Childhood Sexual Abuse in Historical Perspective," Social Science Research Council, July 12, 2012, https://tif.ssrc.org.

110. Jerry Fileau, "50 Years- Evolve: Understanding of Child Sex Abuse," Catholic News Service, February 23, 2004, http://www.bishop-accountability.org.

111. "Home Is Still Key Factor in Juvenile Difficulties," *Denville Herald*, September 24, 1953.

112. Ibid.

113. Ibid.

114. Ibid.

115. "What to Do for a Hall," *Denville Herald*, October 8, 1953.

Chapter 6

116. "Oberg v. Department of Law and Public Safety," Leagle, https://www.leagle.com.

117. "Captain Remembers Back When," *Daily Record*, December 26, 1967.

118. Ibid.

119. "Denville Tp. Accepts Jenkins Resignation: Jeers, Petitions, Fail to Halt Town Fathers," *Daily Record*, August 2, 1962.

120. Ibid.

121. "New Jersey Monthly Ranks Denville among Top 50 Towns in the State," Tap into Denville, August 29, 2019, https://www.tapinto.net.

122. Ibid.

123. "Denville Boys Invited to Organize New Sport Club," *Denville Herald*, September 10, 1953.

124. "New Club for Teen-Age Boys Being Formed," *Denville Herald*, September 17, 1953.

125. Ibid.

126. "40 Boys Organizing PAL," *Denville Herald*, October 1, 1953.

127. "Denville PAL," *Denville Herald*, October 8, 1953.

128. "Denville PAL Swearing in to Be Nov. 7," *Denville Herald*, October 15, 1953.

129. Ibid.

130. "Denville PAL Ceremony," *Denville Herald*, November 19, 1953.

131. Ibid.

132. "PTA Aims for Higher Total Membership," *Denville Herald*, October 22, 1953.

133. "Church Planning Sale of Children's Sport Goods," *Denville Herald*, November 5, 1953.

134. "MYF Doubles Attendance," *Denville Herald*, October 8, 1953.

135. "Denville Township: #13 In Best Places to Live in NJ," Niche, https://www.niche.com.

136. Ibid.

137. Ibid.

138. James Gilbert, *A Cycle of Outrage: America's Reaction to the Juvenile Delinquent in the 1950s* (New York: Oxford University Press, 186), 4.

BIBLIOGRAPHICAL NOTE

A ll of the quotations in this work were spoken by the real people as reported by various newspapers—all extensively cited in the notes section at the end of this book. The following is a generalization of the sources.

Most of the images, unless otherwise noted, come from the Denville Historical Society's collection, namely, the Cobb Collection, the Flormann Collection, the Freeman Collection and the Illig-Viliard Collection. Other images come from various newspapers, with the majority from the *Morristown Daily Record*, where there was a front-page article each day starting from September 1 to September 4, 1953, and then nothing until a small article on September 10. These can be accessed in person at the North Jersey History and Genealogy Center in Morristown, New Jersey.

The re-creation of the events as described in chapter 2, as well as all quoted dialogue that appears there, was pieced together or derived entirely from the following *Morristown Daily Record* articles, which can also be accessed in a hard copy format at the North Jersey History and Genealogy Center in Morristown:

Daily Record. "Hold 2 for Murder; Robbery One Motive." September 2, 1953.

———. "Jury in Denunciation of Juvenile Crime Conditions in County." October 17, 1953.

———. "Man Found Slain in Lover's Lane." August 31, 1953.

———. "13 Denville Youths Held Without Bail in Lover's Lane Murder." September 4, 1953.

———. "13 Held in Denville Murder Case: All Confess to Being at the Crime Scene." September 1, 1953.

———. "13 to Be Arraigned for Murder." September 3, 1953.

The re-creation of the events as described in chapter 3 and the epilogue, as well as all quoted dialogue that appears there, was transcribed entirely from the transcript of proceedings in the Superior Court of New Jersey Law Division—Morris County, New Jersey. *The State of New Jersey vs. George W.C., et al., Defendants*; Courthouse of Morristown, NJ—Monday, November 9, 1953; before honorable Donald M. Waesche, Judge. The files are accessible to the public through an open public records act (OPRA) request to the Morris County Prosecutor's Office. (MCPO OPRA File Number 20-0091).

The transcripts of the Denville Community Church—chapter 4—were pieced together from quotations and stories extensively covered by the *Denville Herald* between September and November 1953. These files can be publicly accessed as PDFs at the Denville Public Library. The following articles are the basis of all quoted conversations:

Denville Herald. "Mail Bag: To the Editor." September 10, 1953.

———. "Recreation Center Seems What Teenagers Want." October 8, 1953.

———. "What Caused This Event." Editorial. September 3, 1953.

———. "Youth Needs Better Parents, Not Curfew." September 10, 1953.

ABOUT THE AUTHOR

Peter Zablocki is a historian, author, teacher and podcaster living in Denville, New Jersey. Focusing on local history, he is the author of *Denville Goes to War: Denville's Story of World War I* and the forthcoming *Denville in World War II*, coming out in March 2021 from The History Press. Additionally, he contributes a monthly column of local history to a town publication, *Denville Life*. He is an Advanced Placement Seminar and Research teacher with over sixteen years of teaching experience. Peter also serves as the vice president of the Denville Historical Society and Museum and is one of Denville's town historians. When not teaching, researching or writing, he can be heard cohosting a weekly podcast, *History Teachers Talking*, with his college friend.

Visit us at
www.historypress.com